Where is your God?

Where is your God?

Michael Paul Gallagher SJ

Darton, Longman and Todd
London

First published in 1991 by
Darton, Longman and Todd Ltd
89 Lillie Road, London SW6 1UD

British Library Cataloguing in Publication Data
Gallagher, Michael Paul
 Where is your God?
 1. Christianity. Faith
 I. Title
 234.2

ISBN 0–232–51919–6

Cover design: Sarah John
Photograph of author: Anne King

Phototypeset by Input Typesetting Ltd, London SW19 8DR
Printed and bound in Great Britain by
Courier International Ltd, Tiptree, Essex

Contents

Introduction: Memories of Encounter

This book is born out of a particular personal situation. After some twenty years teaching literature at University College, Dublin, I am about to move to the Vatican – which will mean a big change. There I am due to work with the Council for Dialogue with Non-Believers. In one sense it may not be so different, because over the years I have enjoyed plenty of dialogue with students, believers and non-believers alike. These pages can be seen as a farewell gift to those I met here in J211 – the office where I am writing and where many an adventure of dialogue has taken place. They are written also in the hope of continuing that conversation at least in print. As life takes me in another direction, I would like to think of this book as reaching some of the people I might have met here, had I stayed on in university work in Ireland.

All those contacts with students – as both lecturer and priest – have given me whatever insights I have into the changing world of beliefs today. It has been a long cross-roads experience. I myself grew up in a smallish village in the West of Ireland in the forties and fifties – before the arrival of so-called modernity. So my roots were traditional and rural. Being thrown into the totally different horizon of university pushed me to ponder what on earth was happening to people in the new culture of today. The students I met had been born into a different world to mine. If I had been born twenty or thirty years later, I wonder if I would now be a priest or even a Catholic. It would certainly have been more difficult. Born into the sixties and seventies, I would have had to cope with much more rootlessness and more complex pressures. A steadiness for commitment would be harder to reach. Or so it seems from what I have learned over those decades.

This book is born from my memories of those years. I want to write about some roads to faith today and I would like to do justice to the tone of that journey as I have heard it in young people I have known. It is not a simple search. It is unique for each person. It will also differ according to the situation around: the notes in the faith-chord struck in Latin America will sound different harmonies to those typical of Europe or North America. In fact my own life brought me into some contact with those worlds. In recent years the biggest influence on my own faith has come from two visits to Latin America (a total of only nine months but they had a major and liberating impact on me). In this book I want to draw on that experience and on the contrasts of faith languages that I have seen. But the principal source for these pages lies in the hours and hours of talking with individuals whom I have been blessed to know over the years, and so a personal note will dominate these pages. Their focus will be the individual search so characteristic of young people in the Western world now. To foster that wavelength of personal reflection, I want to write as if in dialogue with some of my friends. Even as I write, I am thinking of particular people and keeping them in mind should help to preserve an informal and exploratory style. Many of the sections here start from what might coldly be called 'case histories'; for me they are real memories of real people. Sometimes I change the names and sometimes merge stories of different people into one. But I record them all with reverence, and in the hope that they may kindle imagination and courage in others too.

Looking back now at those hundreds of conversations over three decades, I am struck with how privileged I have been and how often those encounters helped to keep my own faith alive. I feel a huge gratitude for the trust of many young people, as they explored various areas of their human experience. Sometimes – but rarely enough – our starting point was religious. More typically we began from something of human struggles – in relationships, in families, in studies, in moods, in the decisions facing them. Frequently there was some trigger of pain that opened the door to searching and to the risk of trusting a comparative stranger. For them it was often a rare experience to be able to speak honestly or to be heard with some understanding, or just to listen to their own unvisited depths. Gradually I came to accept that I had a gift for such encounters: I seemed to have, most of the time at least, some knack of imagination to enter into the experience of people younger than myself and to offer them some space of freedom. But such occasions always came as a surprise and a blessing to me.

As I say, most of our starting points were non-religious, but there was often some religious hunger that found expression later on. I began to realize that this was the natural order of things: we need to be free in our humanity before we can venture into the more mysterious world of our spiritual selves. Being burdened by some hurt can block me from hope. If I am carrying some guilt, it can dent my self-worth and shut me in on myself. I need to reach some clearing in the forest in order to see things more clearly. That is the gift we can be to one another: we can offer an oasis for hearing and healing. And in my experience some such entry into self-freedom is needed before a journey towards explicit faith can be fruitful. That pattern of liberation was a main concern of my book, *Free to Believe: ten steps to faith*.

EMERGING FROM CONFUSION

These pages continue that theme but with a different focus.
Now I want to evoke the experience of arriving at faith and
of living it today. Where previously I tried to explore the
credibility of Christianity, now I am much more interested
in its *livability*. I am thinking less of the unbeliever than the
searching believer or half-believer, less of a journey toward
faith from outside than a journey from confused to more
convinced faith. I am thinking of so many people who were
born into belonging to some Church, but who fall into a
limbo of vagueness along the way. And yet they remain
open to the vision they once glimpsed in Christianity. With
them in mind, this book will try to locate the adventure of
faith within human experience. So it will be less interested
in the contents of the creed than in the journey towards
making basic sense of God for today.

For such travellers I propose the Magi story as a marvellously rich map; in this gospel tale, so often viewed only as
a Christmas story for children, I find a drama of the discovery of faith – as will be explained in the next section.
Thus this book stems from encounters with young people
over some twenty years. It is inspired in its structure by the
Magi story. And it seeks also to draw upon my own experience of different contexts for faith in today's world,
especially the contrasting horizons of Latin America and the
so-called Western world.

The book's title comes from one of the most lyrical passages in the Bible, from Psalm 42. There the poet is suffering
from being far from home, and from the mockery of hostile
people:

> I have no food but tears
> day and night,

> as all day long I am taunted
>   'Where is your God?'

His poem recalls past moments of joyful celebration surrounded by a community of believers. But the past is past.
Here and now, assaulted by the voices of unbelievers, he
feels vulnerable, alone, and longs to see again 'the face of
God' – like 'a deer yearns for running streams'. His prayer-
poem swings between desolation and hope. At times he
senses a kind of 'death in my bones', as if helpless before
the sarcasm of the doubters. But gradually he emerges into
confidence that he will be guided to the 'holy mountain' and
be able once more to find his language of faith.

> Why so downcast,
>   why all these sighs?
> Hope in God! I will praise him still,
>   my Saviour, my God.

The plight of that ancient poet is paralleled in so many ways
today. We live in a time where the basics have shifted and
where faith has gone into a kind of exile. Many people may
have memories of moments and places where faith seemed
alive, when they too, in their own way, went 'to the house
of God among cries of joy'. But the present can seem numb
and blank. How can we emerge into hope like the psalmist?
Only by confronting that same question – 'Where is your
God?' – with something of the same honesty: if we can listen
to it in the tones of today, then we might move towards new
trust for tomorrow. In this book I try to tell how I have
witnessed the struggle of the Psalmist and the hope of the
Magi in lives that I have known.

Many friends have helped me glimpse the various whereabouts of God. Some have helped very practically in the

preparation of this book; my special thanks to Jean van Altena, Donal Neary, John Pringle, and Freddie Quinn.

The Gospel of the Magi

After Jesus had been born at Bethlehem in Judaea during the reign of King Herod, suddenly some wise men came to Jerusalem from the east asking, 'Where is the infant king of the Jews? We saw his star as it rose and have come to do him homage.' When King Herod heard this he was perturbed, and so was the whole of Jerusalem. He called together all the chief priests and the scribes of the people, and enquired of them where the Christ was to be born. They told him, 'At Bethlehem in Judaea, for this is what the prophet wrote:

> *And you, Bethlehem, in the land of Judah,*
> *you are by no means the least among the leaders of*
> *   Judah,*
> *for from you will come a leader*
> *who will shepherd my people Israel.'*

Then Herod summoned the wise men to see him privately. He asked them the exact date on which the star had appeared and sent them on to Bethlehem with the words, 'Go and find out all about the child, and when you have found him, let me know, so that I too may go and do him homage.' Having listened to what the king had to say, they set out. And suddenly the star they had seen rising went forward and halted over the place where the child was. The sight of the star filled them with delight, and going into the house they saw the child with his mother Mary, and falling to their knees they did him homage. Then, opening their treasures, they offered him gifts of gold and frankincense and myrrh. But they were given a warning in a dream not to go back to Herod, and returned to their own country by a different way.

Matthew 2:1–12 (NJB)

The Magi Revisited

Waiting to place the 'wise men' in the crib remains one of my vivid memories of Christmas as a child. They seemed so much more exotic than shepherds. My preference for them, I later discovered, echoed a long history of Christian imagination. The earliest representations of Christmas in the catacombs were of the Magi; the shepherds came later and never attained the same popularity with artists – at least not until the carols of the Reformation. The early centuries meditated at length on that journey of the Magi and wove layers of legend around the simple story as told in Matthew's Gospel.

At first they were portrayed as astrologers with pointed Phrygian caps. The sixth-century mosaics of Ravenna named them, for the first time in the West, as Balthasar, Melchior and Gaspar. About this same time they rose to the dignity of being kings, probably because of the mention in Psalm 72 of kings of Arabia bearing gifts. My favourite example is in the stonework of Autun Cathedral where the three are in the same bed under a large blanket, and all are wearing their crowns! An angel is waking them to point out the star. One of them is shown with eyes wide open in wonder, another half-awake, but the third remains sound asleep – as if to represent three stages of spiritual alertness in the medieval tradition.

In all the early period they were portrayed as identical figures. It is only from the twelfth century onwards that the magi-kings assume individual characteristics, being depicted as the three ages of life, or as representing different races and continents of the world. From this epoch comes a delightful legend that the three met for Christmas Mass in Armenia in AD 54 and that they died happily within a few days, all of them being well over a hundred years old. At some point their supposed bodies turned up in Milan, but after the sack of that city in 1164, Cologne Cathedral managed to acquire the relics and they remain there still in a magnificent enamelled shrine. In the late Middle Ages a Cologne breviary announced that the kings had in fact been consecrated as bishops by St Thomas in India, thereby creating another problem for artists concerning what headgear to give them.

Apart from the legends and the art, spiritual writers reflected on the Magi in many ways. The Venerable Bede was one of those who suggested meanings for the three gifts: gold signified kingship, incense divinity, and myrrh was a prophecy of the Passion. A few centuries later St Bernard's interpretation was more down to earth: money for the poor family; incense to disinfect the stable; and myrrh as a herbal remedy against worms in children. In our own century the tradition continues. Two Nobel-prize winning poets offered rather contrasting angles on conflict at the heart of the story. T. S. Eliot evoked a difficult journey towards a moment of costly inner conversion: this Birth seemed like Death for them, and so disturbed them that they were 'no longer at ease' in their old vision of things. But for the Guatemalan, Miguel Angel Asturias, the white king offers gold in order that Jesus may confront the lure of wealth and power: 'Even from the cradle You may see the Enemy . . . with You is born the grave of Gold.' More recently, Ermanno Olmi, the Italian film director, has developed the Magi story at some length in *Cammina Cammina*, and I shall draw upon his work as an epilogue to this book.

LATIN-AMERICAN INSIGHTS

With that long and fascinating history, one need not feel shy in offering yet another version of the Magi story. I had been pondering it for some years when it came into focus in a powerful way last year in Venezuela. I outlined the story as a theme for reflection and prayer during some retreats for young people. They took up my suggestion and together we began to see this gospel passage as offering a rich agenda of Christian commitment. From their pooling of insights, born of prayer and of listening to one another, these are some of the angles and lights that we hit upon, and which served as inspiration for the chapters which follow here.

The Magi started from seeing a star. To my Venezuelan friends this was a perfect image of anything that calls people to set out on a journey towards faith. Each of us is here to seek and to be faithful to the light that we see. In the drama of Latin America that light is experienced in the cry of the oppressed, in the scandals of history that call for justice. It is also known in quieter and more personal ways, whenever a person realizes that he or she is here for a purpose.

It struck those young people as significant that the Magi had not travelled alone. It symbolized for them a vital element in their own faith, which was so strongly nourished in small weekly gatherings. So following the light and searching for Christ are meant to be a community journey, not a lonely quest.

What about Herod? we asked. Who is he now? *El podoroso*, was one of the replies in the group. The powerful one. The one who controls things and tries to deceive. More dangerous than an outright enemy is the dictator who pretends to be religious but who really wants to kill Christ. In Latin America they are acutely aware of how the Church can be manipulated by governments to stifle the urgency of the gospel. The conclusion of our groups was that some confrontation with Herodian systems is part of being a Christian now.

Eventually the Magi entered 'the house' and 'saw the child with his mother Mary'. We spoke about the places where we find Christ, and about the special role of Mary in Latin-American spirituality. We paused on the idea of the house as a symbol of Church. Where is the real Church experienced today? Many answers flowed: in silence, in suffering, in sacraments, in learning from the poor, in solidarity of vision, in all the struggles of the Kingdom.

One purpose of the journey of the Magi was to offer their gifts. In our reflections this became yet another symbol of the goal of faith: everyone has her or his own gift to bring to the world, for the sake of others.

For all their learning, the 'wise men' were unaware of Herod's duplicity until they had a dream. What could that dream be for us, we asked. It would mean getting in touch with the deepest part of ourselves where the Spirit speaks. It would entail a long discernment of our world, and then a Christian dream for today could be born.

The Magi returned home by 'another way'. In this simple phrase we discovered a final summary of the Christian life. To have found Christ, or to have been found by Christ, leads to measuring things differently. The Kingdom is an alternative vision of what human life is about. It is utterly different from Herod's way of power and ego and death. Instead, it is a life-giving way of serving others, and of letting go of self.

There was depth in the inventiveness of the old legends that grew up around the Magi story. There is equal depth in the intuitions of those Venezuelan communities. This book hopes to expand on those hints and to re-read that gospel story as evoking an adult adventure of faith.

The Star: Awakening to Wonder

What got the Magi going? St Matthew is not forthcoming about that. All that the gospel text tells us is that these astrologers of an Eastern country saw a star in the sky and for some reason set out on a search for the new-born king. But something unusual must have struck those sky-gazers, to spur them into such a risky journey. Something must have awoken their wonder and their hope.

The Bible scholars have much to tell us about the Eastern world and its assumptions, about how there were many learned experts in astrology or astronomy, about how the appearance of a marvellous star in the sky was thought to herald the birth of some great person. And so on. They also suggest that this may be a particular kind of scripture story – called midrash – *where images of faith are more important than historical accuracy.*

The puzzle still remains. Why follow the light? Why set out at all on such a quest? Perhaps answers from our own experience are as valid as any that come from expert research. To seek out the light is a basic image for any religious quest. It is a simple way of capturing what we are here for: to be faithful to conscience and experience, to follow the light we see.

But what opens our eyes to such light? How does the journey get underway?

TRUSTING ONE'S OWN LIGHT

I remember how the journey started for Paul. One day he
came to discuss difficulties over an essay and stayed to talk
about home and parents, about feeling ungrateful, about
not being able to make himself understood. Perhaps pain
was the awakener: it gave him the push to explore his experience, to trust someone else with his situation.

Putting it that baldly is unfaithful to my memory of that
first conversation between us. Set down in such cold words
it seems reductive. What I now recall most clearly is the
relief Paul felt at being able to voice that flood of confusion
inside him. Not that the home situation was one of conflict.
Indeed there was great kindness from everyone there but
he felt burdened by the silence he had adopted. He also felt
guilty about not responding differently. There was a kind of
sadness in him because a gap had opened between him and
his parents, a gap of non-communication. So much had
happened within him these last years – since coming to
university and beginning to think for himself – that it seemed
as if his parents could never grasp his new language. Perhaps
the trouble was that Paul had never before spoken the language of Paul to anyone. That was the breakthrough of our
conversation – and a blessing for both of us. As I listened I
could hear so much goodness – but goodness a bit smothered
under his own self-shadows and doubts.

At one stage I remember saying to him: 'Break the magnifying glass – throw it away.' I told him my theory (to be
taken with a grain of salt) that the devil has a factory somewhere that specializes in manufacturing one thing only, and
something he delights in giving out free. A negative magnifying glass! We took a page of a book and I asked him to
imagine what a magnifying glass does if one holds it over
the middle of the page. It enlarges some lines or words but
it distorts the rest. It was an image of Paul's experience.

Like many others (including myself), he had developed a distorted picture of some of the disappointments of his life. They stood out so much that they prevented him from seeing the whole page, the whole story of his humanity. But the whole page came into view as he grasped the courage to express his negatives for the first time. Paradoxically, negatives made way for positives. The honesty over hurts opened doors to new hope, to seeing himself with some tenderness again. Those hurts, bottled up in self-silence, had come to loom too large for him; so talking it out gently allowed him to trust another side of himself – the hungers and the goodness hidden underneath the numbness.

TWO LEVELS OF FAITH

That first day's conversation was a good day's work for both of us. It was a crucial move into freedom – and so easy really. I have been blessed to see many others take a similar step out of fog into clearing of self-clouds. It seems familiar territory to me now and yet it is always unique. What I am convinced of is that this awakening to the light of one's own goodness often leads – as if naturally – to a more explicitly spiritual journey of faith. Perhaps faith (with a small f) comes before Faith (with a capital F). That first 'faith' is in one's own self as worthwhile in spite of trouble – and it is this self-worth that life often bruises. Looking back now at my years of listening in this very room, I see that I spent a lot of time fostering 'faith' and trusting that 'Faith' might come into focus later on. From my experience I came to believe that the road to 'Faith' usually passes through 'faith'. As indeed it did for Paul. He had to believe again in his own eclipsed goodness before he could begin the stranger adventure of believing again in God. In 'faith' he experienced the human basis of 'Faith'. That was his awakening to light.

Our more explicit entry into Faith-language came from
my mentioning an image from the gospel – the parable of
the hidden treasure. It was as if we both stumbled across
something buried in the field. Imagine someone unearthing
a box under the surface of the soil. At first it can look dirty
and one might fear that it contains just rubbish or even a
dead animal. Then comes the surprise of opening it and
finding something precious. We experienced that discovery
in our listening together, and we also knew something of
the second half of the parable. In Christ's story the person
hides the treasure again – in order to sell everything to be
able to buy the field. Even though Paul began to mention
God that first day, we were slow to enter that realm; it was
as if we were both shy before the treasure found. As someone else in similar circumstances said to me, 'Faith is too
important to rush into until it's ripe'. I could not agree more.
I have learned reverence for the rhythms of people's growth.
The person in the parable went away happy, knowing the
riches within the field – and happy with having to wait until
he or she would be ready to own it one day. We too ended
that first exploration with a sense of gratitude for what had
been already found and of more, much more, yet to come.

Perhaps people often awaken to the light when they have
the courage to speak their pain, and to realize that there is
so much more than the pain. Where there is real listening
the magnifying glass can so easily be broken. Paul saw no
star in the sky. He rode no camels across the desert. But
our conversation echoed the excited intuition that got those
Magi going. It was an awakening into light, and a hunch
that as 'faith' was being born anew in his humanity, Paul
was also entering a larger and Magi-like adventure of 'Faith'.

THE ORPHANAGE AND THE LAKE

Some years ago a student friend of mine surprised me one day with a story he had written. Over the previous months we had spoken a few times about faith. Andrew was going through a fair bit of questioning about religion and about his attitude to church in particular. Looking back now, perhaps much of our talking stayed groping in a world of ideas, whereas what Andrew needed was the freedom of images. Happily he hit upon this level of communication and came up with a parable of his own. I hope that he will publish it in full one day but meanwhile I offer a summary of what I remember of it.

It concerned a little boy – of about ten – growing up in an orphanage. One night in the large dormitory he wakes up in the dark but knows that the dawn can't be far away. It is summer time and there is a lake in the grounds of the orphanage. He feels a great urge to see the dawn at the lakeside but the rules are rigid: on no account should any child get up before the bell and it is strictly forbidden to leave the dormitory until the proper time. But he decides to risk it. He dresses quickly and creeps out, holding his shoes in his hand so as not to wake the others. Then there is a long corridor and – a nice touch – all along this corridor are the pictures of the past presidents of the institution along one side and of saints on the other side. So the boy puts his head down and runs through the long corridor: he does not want his eyes to be caught by the disapproving glances of the figures on the walls. He comes to the lake and waits in darkness for the dawn; sure enough, the drama of day begins, and the colours change from orange to red to bright sun. He watches all this reflected in the water of the lake, absorbed by the sheer beauty of it. Then suddenly he remembers the time. They will be up by now. He will be missed. He will be in trouble. So he gets up to return and

speaks his last words to the lake: 'I'll go back now. Thank
you. I don't care if I'm punished. Because I know something
now – I know that the God of the lake is greater than the
God of the orphanage.'

Over the years I have come back to that story as a simple
but powerful evocation of where many people are as regards
religion. Alas, they may have encountered only the orphanage with its rules and codes and organization. The God of
the orphanage is worshipped in a religion of ritual. But the
God of the lake is encountered in a way that goes beyond
that into something of wonder and awe and freedom. More
and more I am convinced that this is the most neglected
door into faith today. There has been so much of excellent
renewal but has it really touched people on any level of
depth experience? A central struggle for us all is to reach
the hunger and wonder at the core of each person, or as
they say in the East, to get to the cave of the heart where
the Spirit dwells. Or as Paul Tillich used to say, God is the
name we give to an 'inexhaustible depth' within us; and any
entry point to that depth is a potential road to God. It is as
if each one of us is a skyscraper with many floors. But we
leave many of them unvisited. We fall into the habit of
taking the lift to a few limited layers of work, relaxing,
religion – all in somewhat routine fashion. Then wonder
shrivels up, and we miss the moments that might awaken us
for a Magi-like quest. Even the word 'God' can become a
distant and conventional term, one that conjures up a poten-
tate of the universe rather than a passionate and intimate
lover. The real victim of these reductions to routine is our
sense of mystery. If I were asked what is the most critical
religious need today, I would opt for this experience of
mystery, whatever form it might take. Let us get away from
rituals and into imagination, into a poetry that can reach
people's shy hunger. I call it shy because the orphanage has
so often ousted the lake. It is as if the little boy was doing

something shameful in seeking out the space which his heart and imagination needed.

TRUSTING OUR DEPTHS

The spiritual intuition captured in that story can find support among theologians of today. One of my favourites is the Benedictine Sebastian Moore, who has insisted that the ineffectiveness of much organized religion is due to its failure to reach our 'pre-religious God awareness'. By this he means, I think, that the lake experience can be smothered by an over-anxious orphanage. He would hold that God lives in each person prior to our words, beliefs or sacraments. Thus our religiousness of the spirit is deeper than our religion of the Church; ultimately they need each other for a full language of faith.

Karl Rahner also devoted a lot of energy to the crucial experience of mystery. Even the word mystery can be kid-napped by common sense and made to mean something that cannot be understood. In its more genuinely religious meaning it stands for something that is too rich for mere understanding. For Rahner the essential mystery 'is preached to us from within by God'. Therefore the starting-point for any faith journey has to be 'a person's self-experi-ence' at its deepest. It is there that everyone has a basic experience of God if only s/he can recognize it. This is the foundation of religion through the ages, but in today's secu-lar climate this encounter between wonder and mystery is often suppressed. There results a kind of spiritual malnu-trition, or another version of the orphanage forgetting the language of the lake. This is a danger not only in the busy priorities of church life but, on a more academic level, in the neglect of religious experience as a foundation for theology.

How can the lake experience be nourished? Where can we reach this wavelength of wonder? There are many ways

of awakening to the mystery within. Prayer is one –
especially a prayer that trusts the silence. Suffering is
another – when it humbles and opens the heart. Joy is
another – as when a child is born or when fullness is glimpsed
through art or music. Feelings are often our best guides. As
I write, it strikes me that within the last few days I have
three times noticed tears in the eyes of men – a bridegroom
speaking at his wedding, his brother listening to that speech,
and an illiterate drug addict, surprised when a friend praised
his sharp mind and real goodness. These are all moments
of glimpsing the depths of life. But the depths are there
whether we touch them or not. The lake can invite even
during the undramatic everyday.

Perhaps the examples mentioned are a little special. If so,
echoing St Paul I would suggest an even better way: that
wherever love is struggled for and lived, there is the source
of mystery in each life. Love is our lake in the flow of
ordinary existence. What lies behind the faces you see pass-
ing in the street? They may seem tired, preoccupied,
grumpy. But there is so much more. I remember a famous
image in George Eliot's *Middlemarch* where she asks a similar question: 'If we had a keen vision and feeling of all
ordinary human life, it would be like hearing the grass grow
and the squirrel's heart beat, and we should die of that roar
which lies on the other side of silence.' I admire the elo-
quence but my own intuition is more positive. There are
angels at work in each heart. Too poetic? Perhaps. And yet
it is my experience that 'on the other side of silence', in the
depths of people, there is always courage and compassion,
love and longing, even if unsure and inarticulate. Dawn at
the lakeside is not only a moment of beauty in the outer
world; it has its many mirrors in the cave of each heart.

In these and many other ways the 'star' continues to
beckon people. Invitations to wonder awake us. New vistas
open. Risk now seems worthwhile. Thus faith is born when

the ordinary is broken into by the extraordinary. A journey becomes possible into the known unknown. Some of the contours of such a journey will be our focus in the remainder of this book.

Coping with the Dark

Reading between the lines of the Magi story, it seems that their experience was not one of steady light. That star did not appear and then stay shining brightly all along their journey. If that were so, they would not have had to approach Herod and his experts in Jerusalem. Nor would the 'sight of the star fill them with joy' when they saw it again between Jerusalem and Bethlehem.

In brief their experience was what Ruth Burrows has called the 'light-on' light-off' pattern, typical of any faith journey. Everyone runs into painful patches in one way or another. So how can we cope with unsteadiness of light, with the dark times?

Can we walk wisely without the light – or when it seems to have disappeared? Can we insure that darkness does not deflect us from the goal of our journey?

VARIETIES OF BURDENS

I like one of the sayings of Chesterton that faith is the art of surviving one's moods. It rings true in my experience – of myself and of others. There are times when for all sorts of reasons I have practically no sense of God, no taste for prayer, and indeed little desire to do anything about it. I say 'little desire' deliberately, because I think that there has always been a glimmer of hope there, some kind of trust that I will emerge from this cul-de-sac of low spirits.

Other people I have known have had to carry much heavier burdens of desolation than I have ever experienced – the result of family tragedy, or broken relationships, or painful levels of anxiety or depression, or simply due to a blank wall of silence when they try to reach out to God. Why keep going when things seem so pointless? I have often heard some version of that cry and I have no easy answers. Faced with such genuine pain, I am always afraid of being glib, of trivializing what people experience.

But it is good to talk about the various darknesses encountered by people – in their humanity and on the way of faith. These experiences are real; they can frighten and damage a person or else they can purify and give wisdom. Here I want to explore three different experiences of the dark: the everyday darkness of the tired self; the theological darkness at the core of faith; and darkness of the doubting Thomas in ordinary life.

THE TIRED SELF

To begin with, let me borrow an image from my confrère John Powell. I can't remember in which of his books I came across it, but it has stayed with me as a useful parable of what I am calling the tired self – and about the temptation to judge impulsively in the dark. It tells of a man coming back to his house one dark night and seeing a large snake on the lawn of his front garden. He happens to have a hatchet or something of that sort in his car and attacks the snake with it. It writhes and jumps around but eventually is left in bits on the ground. A gory tale. . . . But when the man wakes up next morning and looks out what does he see in pieces all over the grass but the garden hose. Adapting that story to our purposes, the moral would seem to be: if you see snakes in the night, don't fight them; in the morning, they might turn out to be only the garden hose. In other words, we judge badly in the dark and should wait until day. It will come, even after the longest and darkest night. Whenever fatigue of spirit is in the driving seat, it is likely to distort what you see. So beware moods of mere down-ness and wait for the return of light.

It has been a revelation for me to wait with people through deep dark, through times when dawn seemed to have forgot-ten to come. Yet eventually it did come. Self-patience was all. Plus the common sense not to kill imaginary snakes. How often just talking about the desolations can raise a person's hopes! And when they have travelled their Magi-path in their own way and found a sense of God in Christ, they can look back at the darker roads and see them differ-ently. It is as if that ancient psalm had come true:

> My trust does not fail even when I say,
>   'I am completely wretched'.
> In my terror I said,
>   'No human being can be relied on'.
>   (Psalm 116:10–11)

There is a marvellous contradiction there: on one level I trust, while on another I don't. What a person says or experi-ences consciously does not necessarily coincide with their stronger self, the self that can survive through the dark.

DARKNESS OF FAITH

There are darknesses that come from the sufferings of life (and here, as I said, some people seem to carry heavier loads than others) but there is also an unavoidable darkness right at the heart of faith. Here is a true story about this second darkness. At the end of a seminar on faith for teachers, a lady in her fifties came and expressed her grati-tude for the session, which in fact had gone well. There had been a sense of real contact between me and the group. She told me that she had been a teacher of religion for some thirty years but that her own faith had been in a kind of limbo for a long time. She had always taught small children about God as if she had no doubts but, as she put it, the best she could do was to trust the great thinkers who had worked it all out – like Aquinas or Newman. Then she drew closer to me, held my arm in a strong grip and asked, 'Are you *sure* there is a life after death?'

It was a bit terrifying to be put, even temporarily, into the same category as Aquinas or Newman. My first answer was to reach for yet another authority: I reminded her of St Paul's strong statements that if the dead are not raised, then Christ was not raised and faith is empty, or again that if our hopes as Christians are limited to this life alone, we deserve to be looked on as fools (1 Cor 15:15–19). But this text was familiar to her and, understandably, was not the answer she wanted. 'But are *you* sure?' she persisted. What could I say? If I said yes, it would be untrue. If I said no, it would be untrue in another way. Yes could mean a provable God, a verifiable faith, both of which seem to me to be contradictions: I have no direct data on God or on the after-life, and the only 'data' I have on the Resurrection of Jesus come from witnesses I have never met and via texts that cannot be checked historically in the usual way.

So I am not *sure* in the normal way of being sure. As Newman once said: 'Religious light is intellectual darkness.' Or to return to images of the Magi story, the light of the star that beckoned them was not comprehensible in terms of the logic of their science: it spoke to them not irrationally but beyond their usual reasonings. This is a way of saying why I could not unhesitatingly and honestly answer yes. My intellect in its usual way of knowing is not 'sure' of God. God is not provable in the everyday sense of proof.

Why, then, not say a blunt no? Because that too would

be misleading. It might suggest that I am living with per-
petual doubt rather than faith. And faith is a strange kind
of knowing. It is always a mixture of fragility and firmness,
of incompleteness and fulfilment. It involves unsureness and
sureness at one and the same time. Its sureness is not of the
usual objective kind: when the first Sputnik was sent into
space, Khruschev boasted that the astronauts found no god
in heaven. But there is another kind of certainty, more akin
to the unshakeable trust than can exist between friends than
to the analysable proofs that take place in laboratories or
through looking around the heavens.

THE NORMALITY OF DOUBTS

Perhaps there is another angle that can be brought in here.
People often surprise me with their surprise that I, a priest,
should experience unsureness about faith. They seem to
think that ordination gives some grace of steady certitude,
of armour-plating against difficulties. Alas, no. For me,
brushes with darkness are normal; at times they are deeply
confusing and painful. I see no point in hiding this. Often I
find myself feeling that the whole 'faith thing' is utterly
unreal. In certain moods I find myself buffeted by doubts
about everything connected with God or Christ or Church
or religion. God seems an impossibility, a tempting illusion
cooked up over the centuries, born out of human needs and
surrounded with a lot of impressive wisdom and admirable
generosity of spirit. Christ surely existed but this extraordinary individual was later interpreted by religiously excited
people in strange ways: a myth built up around a visionary
healer. The Church often seems a prison of dishonesty, and
the real miracle is that so much mediocrity does not alienate
more people from it. The whole history of religion seems
linked with blind fanaticism, violence, rigid attitudes and
hostility to those who break new ground or live creatively.

Yes, I can suffer from dark thoughts and negative judgements. So why not throw in the sponge? Why remain rooted – or try to remain rooted – in faith and in the Church? Negatively because those dismissive postures always arise when I find myself *standing outside* the life of faith, staying at a distance, literally alienated. That is where doubting Thomas is so fascinating as a patron saint. It is surely relevant that he was absent when the Risen Lord showed himself on Easter Day. Whenever I miss some worthwhile experience, and especially if it is my own fault, I am inclined to cover my disappointment by dismissing the significance of what others have found, even if it is only a good film or a celebration of some kind. When Thomas missed the Lord's appearance to the others, he seems to have raised his conditions: 'Unless I put my hands into his side . . .'. At the root of such doubting is a sulking child within. Thomas had been left outside. Not until he could return to the inside, to a sense of relationship with Jesus, would he stop his negatives and voice his cry of returning faith: 'My Lord and my God'. Everyone has Thomas-style moments of doubt, and like him they can stem from a mixture of reactions: being annoyed with oneself; finding the witnesses incredible; and then making exaggerated demands of objectivity.

So I have learned not to trust the sulking self. And, more positively, I have come to recognize that reverence is a key to faith. I may have to wait through dark moods before being able to re-enter that reverence. I may have to put up with myself as I stand sulking outside. But eventually I get in touch again and rediscover a wisdom that is in tune with my deepest human experience. I have stopped being surprised by my bouts of doubt. They come and go like the Irish weather; indeed, they are very much linked with inner weather. My prayer becomes that great phrase of King Lear: 'Sweeten my imagination.' Which means waiting for the return of light. Whenever I am in touch with love, with the giving self, with the goodness of people even in darkness, then faith makes sense. It remains unsure to the Thomas-like me who stands outside; it becomes sure to the me who stands inside the circle and seeks to live its vision.

Only in that way can I give a full answer to the urgent question of that teacher. It is neither yes nor no. It depends on where you are, or on how you are. A sure yes at times. An unsure yes at times. But the yes wins. It sounds a deeper music. It stems from a larger freedom of heart. It gives rise to a more generous living. Even though the storms are real when they come, the yes of faith can survive those storms of being unsure. It can navigate through the fog without undue panic.

Just as the Magi did not always see the star, so unsureness is a common reality for everyone at times. Many people sit uneasy with official clarities, even if they seldom voice their doubts. One woman friend of mine describes herself as a bit of a Buddhist in her Christianity, in that she prefers not to be too clear about God. There is Someone she meets in meditation, but he or she has no face – and sometimes seems more an Absence than a Presence. This same friend stayed away from the sacraments for years, in part, because she felt their language was too definite for her. She remained an honest questioner, never quite at home with official religion and its usual expressions. I think there are many like her who have at least temporary periods of healthy unease with what she calls the 'cocksure language of church'. The mystery of God is more strange by far than the many black and white words pronounced from altars on Sunday.

How then, in practice, can we cope wisely with the dark? St Ignatius Loyola offered a few classical suggestions in his *Spiritual Exercises*, when speaking of surviving through times of desolation. His advice could be boiled down to three maxims.

1: Don't change your course in the dark.

2: Push in the opposite direction to your negative moods.

3: Trust that this empty time will not last.

And this can translate perfectly into the story of the Magi.

1: They kept going, even when the journey seemed a madcap quest, and when they lost the clarity of their initial light.

2: When the star was not guiding them, they looked for help; in other words, they acted against any inclination to abandon the adventure.

3: Their perseverance was rewarded by the return of the star, so that they emerged from confusion into clarity again.

Viewed in this way darkness can be a friend of faith. The absence of steady light is inevitable on any journey of meaning; indeed it forces us to admit the strange experience that is faith, as a unique mixture of fragility and of strength, of doubt and certitude.

Asking Questions: A Dialogue

For such a short story, Matthew's account of the Magi mentions many occasions of questioning. The Magi arrive in Jerusalem and ask 'Where is the infant king of the Jews?' Next Herod asks his group of experts 'where the Christ was to be born', and he later interrogates the Magi as to the 'exact date on which the star had appeared'.

To ask questions is one of the basic human activities. It starts with a child's cascade of daily inquiries and continues in different and deeper ways through life.

A faith without questions may have existed serenely in simpler cultures but today it is almost unthinkable. There are many basic questions about religion today, and it is a time of more questions than answers. To do justice to them requires the right wavelength – a reverence that goes beyond mere argument.

MARRIAGE PREPARATION

Richard and Marian were both ex-students of mine and I was delighted when they asked me to perform their marriage. When we met to plan the ceremony, all went well until we ran into the question as to whether they both wanted to receive communion. I knew Marian to be a firm believer and weekly communicant, but I had never discussed religion with Richard. He seemed embarrassed by the communion question but inclined to say yes. When he told me that he had been out of touch with church practice for several years, I suggested that to come to a good decision over communion might need more time than this quick conversation, which was inevitably focussed on the practicals of the ceremony. I proposed a longer chat, saying that it might be one of the few moments in his life when he had the opportunity to take stock of his religious situation.

Without any hesitation, Richard agreed to meet me at greater length, saying that the whole area of faith had been dormant for years and yes, in his view it needed attention now. So we met for what turned out to be a most enjoyable conversation, which left both of us feeling grateful. Indeed our exchanges seemed so worthwhile that I wrote them down afterwards and developed the text as a wedding gift for both of them. Here is a version of our communion dialogue.

M: Tell me something of what we might call your faith story, about what God meant for you at any time, or about how it changed.

R: That's easy enough. I think I believed in God without difficulty until about 13 or 14, and then it very simply collapsed. Fairly quickly in fact. I could not reconcile the idea of God creating the world with all the new ideas I was picking up from science.

M: So it was an intellectual crisis of a kind.

R: Yes, in so far as a young teenager can have an intellectual crisis. It was not a painful crisis really. I just stopped believing in God the way I had been brought up to do.

M: How did it come about? Did anything in particular happen to trigger your doubts?

R: It was mainly in my own thoughts. I didn't express it very much, except in religion class and there it got me into trouble. At least the teacher responded to my questions with a certain amount of sarcasm. So I shut up.

M: The questions were shot down. Were you hurt by that?

R: Oh sure. But I don't think that was the key to my not believing. I think I just gave up trying to find answers and decided the whole faith thing was for children.

M: Like Santa Claus. Something you grow out of. Something you find out was a fiction for small kids.

R: Exactly – and with as little sense of pain as about Santa Claus.

M: Was there no difficulty at home – if you stopped going to Mass for instance?

R: I didn't stop immediately. I gradually went less and less. Most of my peers were doing the same. Besides my parents weren't pushy about practice, unlike some of the others.

M: So it was mainly internal. God became incredible because of science. I take it that you stopped any personal prayer.

R: That disappeared in time. In fact the whole religion thing went blank for me until last week. I sometimes had discussions with friends but they were just arguments on the surface. Nothing disturbed my 'blankness', my absence of questions, until the issue of communion at the wedding came up.

M: I'm glad we didn't gloss over that. I think it's right to look for what might be the right or honest decision there. It sounds to me as if your faith needle got stuck fairly early in life and hasn't had a chance to move since. You've had no moments when you thought of re-examining the God question for yourself?

R: Not really. Someone like you – a priest and all – might not realize how rare it is to have the right wavelength to raise these things.

M: Perhaps we have it now.

R: I think we have. What do you think about my story, as you called it?

M: Perhaps a mixture of the unusual and the usual. I think it's usual for people of your generation to go fairly blank on God. It's more unusual to do so without pain and so early and over something that could have been answered.

R: How would you answer it now?

M: Partly I'd say that 'now' is different to then. At 23 you're rather different in yourself to what you were at 14. I think you're able to approach the whole issue of faith more maturely. It's a personal question – which is not to say that it simply depends on what you feel. I mean that it's a question that involves how you see your life. To believe in God is a personal business, not just a matter of proving a First Cause for the universe. It sounds as if you got caught in that second agenda out of the sheer thrill of learning to think for yourself. Was science very exciting for you then?

R: Engrossing. Fascinating. A whole new world.

M: It seemed to explain everything.

R: It did then.

M: And now?

R: It's not the same. It's important but there are other things.

M: Like . . . ?

R: Like falling in love and getting married.

M: A whole new world – to quote yourself! And it changes the wavelength we were talking about.

R: How do you mean?

M: I mean that you are able to wonder about faith in a much richer way now. The only God you could believe in or not believe in at 14 was an Explanation for the World, a kind of theorem. But the only God worth believing in is someone utterly different from that: what the Old Testament calls the God of Abraham, of Isaac, of Jacob. In other words a God of persons. Or what the New Testament calls the God who is love. You're now able for that vocabulary – of persons and of love. Because you have experienced it in your own way with Marian. Doesn't that make a big difference?

R: It's the biggest thing that has ever happened to me. I suppose it must change the way I think about everything.

M: Including God?

R: I hadn't really been thinking about God until this conversation. All these years it was a no-go area, not in the sense of anything forbidden or rejected, but simply dead. Something avoided.

M: Did you believe you had solved the question of God at 14? In the negative, I mean.

R: Not really. I stopped wondering about it. I shelved it as impossible, and I was able to live without God, quite easily in fact.

M: And now? even as we talk?

R: It might become real again, or in a new way. I'm surprised at how I'm feeling. Perhaps I'm closer than I thought to faith.

M: In what way, would you say?

R: A bit like you said there now. I know more about life than I did at 14. I'm less in the head. I believe in the personal now and in the possibility of love. If there is a God, he won't be found as some cold explanation of everything.

M: Go on. God will be found as . . .

R: A person you might love.

M: Or a person who might love you. Perhaps that comes first.

R: Why do you say that? I was always taught that you had to love God.

M: There is something crucial we haven't touched on yet. Or more accurately someone. Can you guess?

R: Jesus Christ, I suppose.

M: Exactly. What, if anything, does he mean to you?

R: I'm vague on that. I have a jumble of pictures in my

head – like an art gallery! But I don't know what it adds up to: just old photos, or dim memories.

M: Memories of what?

R: Childhood I suppose. When I used to pray to Jesus. When he was a kind of friend.

M: You had a sense of Jesus as friend before that crisis broke at 14. Can you remember your first communion?

R: Clearly. At least the externals of the day, dressing up in white and all that.

M: And communion itself? did it mean much to you?

R: It was important in some way I can't explain, in a way I've lost touch with now. It was like having a special friend. I would never be alone. But I couldn't return to that now. It's too simple.

M: Yes and no. You've grown up. The images of childhood won't meet your needs now. But what you glimpsed at your first communion could have its truth still. Jesus as a friend who comes. Or as I was saying, a God who loves you. It may sound too simple but it's at the heart of any personal faith. Otherwise you get stuck with some sub-Christian or pagan God – you can't pray to an Ultimate Explanation. You don't receive the First Cause in communion.

R: What do you believe you receive in communion?

M: What Jesus gave at his Last Supper. From all the gospel accounts of that meal, it was an evening when Jesus wanted to give of himself totally. A kind of farewell gift. He spoke of sharing his own peace and joy with his disciples; he promised to send them his Spirit to be within them; he gave them a new command – to love as he had loved them, and as he had symbolized for them in washing their feet. As if to crown all this sharing, he took bread and wine and said – perhaps you remember the words yourself?

R: This is my body. This is my blood.

M: Yes, but there is more. Other words that make all the difference, I think.

R: I don't remember any more. Just the claim that this bread was his body, which is something I've found impossible to believe.

M: The second half can make it more possible to believe. Jesus breaks the bread and gives it to them saying 'this is my body *which will be given up for you*'. The breaking looks forward to the next day and the Cross. The whole purpose of his self-giving is for others. You can't appreciate communion unless you see how it is in tune with all the self-giving by Jesus at that last supper, and indeed in his whole life.

R: You mean the communion bread is a symbol of self-giving rather than what people call 'real presence'?

M: We're getting into deep water there. No, I would not see them as alternatives. Communion is both the presence of Jesus and a symbol of what he was to do the next day. There is no greater love, he said, than to lay down one's life for one's friends. In this spirit he gave himself in bread and wine at the Supper just as he was going to do on the Cross. And of course he added, 'do this in memory of me'. What 'this' are we to 'do', would you think?

R: Say these words. Say the Mass. Give communion.

M: Any other possibility that you see?

R: I don't know. Perhaps imitate what you were stressing there, his whole gesture of self-giving.

M: Exactly. If we forget that central gesture of love, we miss the core of that Last Supper. We reduce it to ritual, or make it seem like magic. If we just perform his actions without trying to live his way, we make Mass into hollow pietism. And I'm afraid that often happens – for myself included on many a dull, routine day. It's hard in experience to grasp the full riches of the eucharist, or to do it justice in practice. So where does all this leave you? We've covered a lot of ground. Perhaps too much. We started off talking about faith itself, and that led to the question of communion. From there we got into the need to live the surrender of

Jesus, and now we're wondering how our celebration of Mass can do justice to the mystery of the Last Supper. Where are we, do you think?

R: I'm learning a lot, although I'm a bit lost too. It's all very interesting. More than interesting, it's opening my eyes to things. I don't know if I can take it all in just yet, or if I can believe it all. But it certainly changes the picture of faith that I had, or the sense of communion that I was starting from.

M: Describe the differences a bit. What has come into focus for you as we've been talking?

R: A good few things. Perhaps the most important would be a challenge to my old agenda about God. I was probably a bit childish in throwing out God just because I could not square his existence with my teenage enthusiasm over science. I see that I might be more ripe for exploring faith now – because it's more a personal thing than an objective thing. I've grown through new experiences in my own life, most of all the experience of love. So I can approach the question of God differently now.

M: What's the main change in approach there?

R: Probably that I should not expect a clear proof for God and that I should not abandon the search because that kind of certainty is impossible.

M: And more positively . . . ?

R: That's harder to pinpoint. If there is a God, he meets me in a very personal way. I suppose that's where Christ would come into the picture.

M: And does he for you now?

R: I can't say. I'd need time to let all this sink in a bit more. You've no idea how new all this is for me. These are things I haven't thought about ever before.

M: If you remain unsure about Christ and faith in him, can you decide to receive communion? That, after all, was our starting-point.

R: It's not so much that I remain unsure. It's that I'd have to ponder over it a bit. I'd certainly like to be able to receive communion. I liked how you were explaining it as Christ's gift of himself at that Last Supper, and how it summarized all he stood for. What do you think I should do?

M: I'd trust your own feeling – that you need time to think, space to let all this sink in. Except I'd open it into the possibility of prayer.

R: I should say some prayers?

M: That's not what I said. If, as you say, you give time to wondering where you are in all this, that could become a reaching out to God – and that's prayer.

R: How could that happen? I haven't prayed for years.

M: I'm not sure what would help you most. Could it be that you're not alone in all this? Could you pause and listen in quiet for the invitation of the Spirit? Because I believe that the Spirit of God is within you. Or you might find Scripture a road to prayer. If you took one of the communion passages and let it become personal. For instance, where Jesus says 'I am the bread of life; no one who comes to me shall ever be hungry'. If Jesus is God, then those words are spoken for you as much as for their first hearers. He's speaking about himself as meeting all your longing as well as about the gift of communion. But I can't teach you to pray. I can only encourage you to listen in your own way, and to be open to finding yourself spoken to by God.

R: That sounds a big step for me – at least from where I have been for so long.

M: It's a step that countless thousands have taken each in his or her own way. 'Seek and you will find.' I think the moment is ripe. But you have to be free. Real faith is always born out of a deep freedom.

R: You may be right. I'll try to give it a chance these days. Perhaps the trouble before was that I was never free about religion, and never realized that it needed another kind of listening, another kind of searching.

M: Or that you might be searched for by God.

R: That would be a surprise, but let's see over the next while – some surprises are true.

Travelling Together: Community

It is always assumed that the Magi numbered three but in fact the gospel does not say this. It simply mentions three gifts, on the basis of which, tradition has usually supposed three givers of those gifts. Sometimes the artists have shown more than three – up to twelve – but gradually it became a convention to depict them as one elderly man, one younger man and one non-white.

What is clear from the text is that there was more than one of them and that they travelled together. In fact there were two groups of people who recognized and welcomed Jesus at his birth – the shepherds and the Magi. Interestingly, one group was from nearby, Jewish, caring and simple people, who did not expect anything special. The others were from far away, non-Jewish, and more conscious searchers after wisdom.

Community seems the normal birthplace and home for faith. So we might now ask, what is the role of companionship with others on this road of searching? And what is happening to our togetherness in the contemporary world and the contemporary church?

SOCIAL CHANGES

Quite recently I found myself called on to help a young man, one of my neighbours in the high-rise flats of Ballymun. At twenty-two he had never had steady employment, and as a result remained withdrawn and shaky in his self-confidence. Yet I knew him as a deep and interesting person to talk with. On this particular occasion he asked me for a reference for a job, which I was happy to give him; we also filled out the application form together. When he was leaving, he turned and said, 'You've been very good to me'. My first impulse was to reply with a conventional 'Not at all'. But I paused and found myself voicing a fuller truth: 'I hope so, but it takes two to make goodness.' In other words, we need others to awaken the goodness that is in each of us, and to bring it out into the open. We are here in this world for one another, even if it is rare to admit that basic truth openly and simply. Paradoxically, we grow by giving. We receive by sharing. We stay alive by little dyings for the sake of one another. And this is true not only in daily kindnesses between people, such as a job reference (the one in question actually worked!), but in the large-scale project of healing this divided and troubled planet. It must be obvious by now that behind these pages lie many experiences of one-to-one encounter. Where would any of us be in our humanity without the wonder and trust born from friends, and from glimpsing their mystery and richness? Yeats's poem 'The Municipal Gallery Revisited' tells of him looking around at the portraits of many whom he had known in his life and the poem ends, 'and say my glory was I had such friends'.

Such companionship is central to most people's lives. Yet there is a larger circle of travelling together and one that is crucial for faith: how we belong with one another in communities of various kinds. Of all that determines how people see their lives differently today than they did in the past, nothing has had more impact than the changes in how we live together. Less than two centuries ago the whole world lived in a rural rhythm. Now the world is predominantly urbanized, with vast numbers living side by side with people they do not know. Where do we truly belong any more? With whom do we find belonging? These questions no longer have easy or automatic answers. This is all the more true of the rich world, in which wealth has paid for fences, security systems, and space which isolates the private property of the self, or that unit called the nuclear family. Volumes have been written about this but the core fact is that people have lost one form of belonging together without finding any genuine alternative.

There is no point in being nostalgic about those older community supports or in dreaming that they could possibly return. A certain world is dead for ever. What is vital is to recognize the price paid in human terms for our modernity: this shift from a society of belonging to a society of anonymity has changed how we image our humanity. One result is that faith has become something private, even for many believers, as well as marginal as a force within Western culture. Indeed this crisis of faith today is largely a by-product of how we live together, or rather how we do not live together. A death of community lies at the origin of much so-called unbelief or alienation from Church or loss of a sense of the spiritual. Remembering the Magi plot again, if Herod can kill belonging or community he may not need to kill Christ.

It is also that a hunger for new community is one of the hallmarks of our time. Sometimes that hope lies dormant, suppressed by our urban addictions to spending, movement, novelty, and so on. But this need has become an urgent quest for many who awaken to the ravages of Herod's rule. They sense that being a Christian cannot be a solitary journey, that faith has never flourished except where community exists in one form or another. If the older languages of belonging – in both society and Church – have collapsed, then new ways of travelling the road together must be found. It is one of the most exciting aspects of church life today that community is being re-discovered – with rich variety and in many places. Perhaps of all the faith dimensions suggested by the Magi story, this travelling together has become the most crucial in today's world. There are other important strands such as imagination, social alertness, prayerfulness, generosity, or commitment, but without a living community, faith is in danger of remaining merely private, and therefore stunted. In the image of the sower parable, where faith lacks social roots, it may wither under the scorching sun (Matthew 13:6).

COMMUNITY OF BROKENNESS

In this light I want to offer here a few eye-witness accounts of how the hunger for community has been met in different ways. My first example of how travelling together can be life-giving comes from my contacts over a few years with Narcotics Anonymous – or N.A. to use their familiar short form. Indeed this privileged experience with ex-addicts has forced me to see the issues more starkly and to admit less grudgingly my own need for community – something that by temperament I tend to neglect. The next two paragraphs were written after returning from an N.A. retreat, and I print them untouched in order to give a sense of my gratitude to these friends and to convey something of the unique community into which they welcomed me.

It's not often that I come home after midnight and have the urge to write instead of go to bed. But it happened tonight. Not for the first time I find myself both stunned and refreshed by the sheer honesty of humanity that I find in N.A. They are all young people who have hit bottom through drugs. All of them remain fragile inside, vulnerable from their experience, haunted by memories and guilt. But my overall sense of them is one of Resurrection, of new life. Out of darkness and evil and 'shit', as they

say, is born feelowship (that started as a typing error but
let it stand) – it is a fellowship of shared feelings with
nothing soft about it.

There is something of transparent authority about
people who have come through so much suffering. It is
hard to identify or describe. Is it a kind of wisdom born
of woundedness? Or a courage of down-to-earth-ness? Or
an absence of the usual games, masks and defences of us
less broken ones? It may seem strange that being broken
can lead to such depth and life. Perhaps because they
were dangerously hooked on an illusion, they can see
through other surface games that distract people from
their real selves. The rest of us avoid humbling experiences, unless they are forced upon us. Some moments
leave us exposed or ashamed, but if we raise our shields
fast enough, nobody will notice, and then we can forget.
We are born evaders of weakness. We are polished pre-
tenders in our pride. We are experts in dodging our essential poverty and therefore the more costly avenues of grace
come to seem unnatural to us.

What I witnessed with N.A. cuts through all that nonsense
– and it is nonsense, literally, non-sense. These people are
in touch with their hungers because they are in touch with
their hurts. They have stepped outside the conspiracy of
half-truth or untruth that so often dominates our 'normality'
– to the extent that we do not know the lies we live. Because
they have hit rock bottom and come through, there is a
directness in their emotions and an openness about their
need for one another. Their addiction was an experience of
profound isolation; but they have emerged from it through
the discovery of community. In this way they have seen
through one of the key heresies of our culture – namely,
that standing on one's own feet is the only way to live, and
that dependence on others is some kind of weakness or

immaturity. When they abandoned this inherited stance of isolation, they found the healing space that is community, solidarity, friendship, support. They know now how crazy it was – and is – to think that we can dispense with sharing the road with others. In our world individualism presents itself as the unquestioned path, but in fact it is a blinkered vision, and another kind of addiction.

This addiction to the private self has come home to me in my other rather different world of university. Discussing literature in a tutorial group, students assume that 'character' is *the* vital question in novels or plays. They have been brought up on a diet of personal consciousness (as was I a generation back). But they seldom see through the subjectivism lurking in this. Nor do they suspect that they could be victims of a culture that makes the self into an idol or that keeps their morality stuck on a childish level of 'if it feels OK, do it'. Recently in a tutorial I remarked that for the majority of the human race these assumptions about the self do not hold, that in the Third World a sense of community is stronger than this ferocious sense of the individual. I was not claiming that there is no egoism in the *barrios* of Latin America – far from it – but that individuals there do not have the same inflated sense of their own importance nor suffer from the radical aloneness imposed on people by our Western life-patterns. In similar fashion, the modern university often leaves its students disillusioned. Where they had hoped for wisdom and friendship, often they encounter only cleverness and competition. Thus the university becomes a microcosm of the First World as a whole: with all its advantages, it ends up condemning people to situations of non-relationship, and this imposed solitude can in turn stifle their sense of God.

By contrast, the discovery by my friends in N.A., born from tragedy and pain, is that it is impossible to survive without community. In this respect, what they and other groups are doing is counter-cultural; they are seeking something that is too basic to be put on sale in Herod's supermarket. In those N.A. members I see the gospel's 'poverty of spirit' in so many forms: in the joy of having come through the horrors and found friends who know the road; in honesty over failure; in the absence of silly pride and in presence of a good-humoured acceptance of each other; and above all, in the willingness to admit hurt and then to care for one another as they travel the road together.

FAITH FRIENDS

I have chosen to give pride of place to the N.A. community experience, because it seems a powerful and transparent example of a basic point, namely that any Magi-like search for wisdom is bound to remain weak unless it finds the unique strength that lies in community. Thus, within the anonymity that is modern society, the contemporary Church is learning to create gatherings of believers, people who come together to support one another in searching for the gospel vision now.

For instance, over the past two years, it has been a special pleasure for me to be involved in a 'faith friends' group of young adults, all of them from Ballymun where, as already mentioned, I have been living in a small Jesuit community. The group first gathered in late September and then met each Monday night until about April, when they went out in pairs to share what they had found with children preparing for Confirmation. Although everyone knew from the outset that the group would eventually serve this purpose with the 'Confirmation kids', practically no mention of this arose until about March. Instead all these months were spent in an unpredictable adventure of human and spiritual discovery, where the members themselves set the agenda. Each week, with help from the priest leading the programme (I was

more a visitor or assistant), they would decide on a topic
for the following Monday. It could be anything, from the
image of Ballymun as a 'problem area' to the experience of
being an unmarried parent, from drawing one's image of
God, and explaining it, to reflecting together on what blocks
us from being our real selves with others. It was exciting to
watch the development of warmth and trust among the
group, predominantly male in fact, and drawn from such a
tough area. The shy ones turned out to be not so shy after
all. The 'hard' ones turned out to be imaginative and 'soft'.
In religious terms the non-practising and unbelieving ones
turned out to have deep hungers and real questions.

At some stage before Christmas, the group started to end
each evening with an exercise in guided silent meditation.
It was a total novelty for most of those present and proved
a marvellous breakthrough for them. Lasting about twenty
minutes, it usually involved some stillness exercise leading
into a fantasy, and finished with a prayer. After Christmas
the discussion topics tended to be more explicitly religious:
Bible, Church, Mass, prayer, the Holy Spirit and so on. By
this stage such an excellent spirit had been built up within
the group that people who would not normally talk about
spiritual issues found themselves free to speak their questions and voice their inner selves. I recall with relish the
good humour with which one man reported that he had been
praying without knowing it! He described how, as a result
of the capacity for quiet learned from the periods of group
meditation, he found himself one afternoon staring out of
the window at the rain for a long time; but instead of it
being a waste of time or an empty dream it was a moment
of attentive wonder, with a sense of God behind it all.

The success of this group was that it opened up new levels
of expression for people who had been limited by a narrow
vocabulary for their humanity and their faith. The sheer
happiness of the weekly meetings was a great experience of

community and of mutual enjoyment. Looking back at the
evolution of trust in the group, it seems proof of the need
to start from people's lived realities if one is to arrive at a
genuine faith language for today. First we had established a
basis of friendship and of human sharing. Then we became
more ambitious and personal in the areas we took for reflection. Next we opened a door to an experience of interiority
through the exercises in meditative quiet. And this led to a
Ballymun version of 'theology from below': a way of understanding issues of faith as arising from human experience.
This rooting of our reflections in life was a slower road of
learning, but a much more fruitful one for those involved
than any jumping to the level of doctrines could have been.

Moreover, for me, this participation in that Faith Friends
group brought about something of a conversion to community. I saw again why, in modern pastoral thinking, so
much stress is put on small communities as key places for
growth in faith. Trust and truth together seem rare in our
urban societies. But if such basic human hungers are trivial-
ized and starved, they do not disappear. They emerge read-
ily and eagerly whenever real nourishment is on offer. It
was certainly exciting to witness those young adults discovering and creating a weekly oasis of community within our
high-rise jungle of flats.

MARRIAGE AND CELIBACY

At the opposite end of the social scale, I have also been
chaplain for several years to a group of married couples
belonging to the Teams of Our Lady. This international
body, which originated in France just before the Second
World War, now exists as a Catholic movement of couples
throughout the world. A team is a small community, usually
up to seven couples, who meet monthly with a chaplain.
Following the insights of the movement's founder Henri

Caffarel, the focus is on a spirituality rooted in the experience of married love. At the start Fr Caffarel found that many couples were leading parallel lives of private religious duties, without ever voicing their faith with one another. The Team's way of life stresses a spiritual journey that is spoken of and shared. Our monthly meetings were held in the homes of each family in turn and began with a meal, the preparation of which was shared out in advance. After this rather French but pleasant start, the remainder of the meeting was given to hearing one another at some depth on the important happenings of each family as well as on the various commitments of our team spirituality: daily personal prayer, reading of Scripture, a monthly 'sit-down' or special listening to one's spouse, and some 'rule of life' or growth point which each individual chooses for herself or himself. Later on we always had some period of guided silent prayer, leading into some sharing of prayers by everyone, and the last part of the evening was devoted to the 'study topic', usually some religious book which we had undertaken to work through, chapter by chapter, pooling and discussing our responses with one another. Thus a fair bit of ground was covered in the three or so hours of the monthly meeting.

Describing the Teams in this way may be necessary for those who do not know the movement, but it totally fails to capture its spirit as a community experience. One member of our team came closer when he said, 'I don't think I would still be a real Catholic without the Teams'. He felt that under all the pressures of modern life, he would have lost his spiritual bearings had it not been for two gifts found through the movement: the companionship with other couples as well as the stimulus to growth in faith. The Team that I was with was always five couples, of middle-class background and mostly with children in their teens or older. This too was a genuine experience of community, less dramatic and less intense than Narcotics Anonymous or the

Faith Friends, but equally real in its slower rhythm of travelling together through the years. The couples found it a
source of great support in times of tension as well as in the
dry and routine patches of life. Together we have carried
one another through moments of serious illness and bereave-
ment, and through anxiety about children and their choices;
at times we have shared with one another our struggles and
personal burdens, and this has often proved a unique safety
net in times of darkness. And we have also celebrated
together moments of success and joy. What now seems
impressive, looking back on some twelve years together, is
that each couple has been able to find nourishment through
the community of the team. It is one more verification of
the fruitfulness of such anchors in today's society; without
them many people suffer from a malnutrition of both
humanity and faith.

For me, involvement with the Teams brought insights into
both marriage and celibacy that I might not have reached
otherwise. I heard couples describe the shock experienced
during the first years of marriage as two previously independent selves had to adjust first to one another, then to
children, and later to all the ups and downs of family life.
And I began to wonder whether the demands of marriage
were not harder to live with than the demands of priesthood.
Both callings are meant to lead to freedom for love, but my
fear is that priesthood can more easily side-step the challenge and so fall short of the real reason for celibacy. As a
priest, I can function quite caringly within the armour of
a role, but without any lasting erosion of my egoism, or
fundamental conversion of heart.

No doubt a similar evasion is possible within marriage.
Yet watching the tough yet happy letting go that marks the
lives of married friends, I feel challenged over the quality
of my love and over the quality of my nourishing that love
in the silence of prayer. Their sacrifices, lived day in, day

out, remind me of the call at the core of celibacy, if it is to be fulfilled and happy. It is a call to some contemplative space where the heart can learn from God. The trouble is that I can shirk entering that space without anyone knowing, whereas if my married friends shirk their family relationships, their doing so is much more evident to all concerned. Celibacy becomes dangerous, I think, when it lacks prayerful listening; for then it loses touch with its main justification, which is mystical. Years ago I used to be more content with a functional view of celibacy – the claim that without family commitments, I can be free for people. But both my experience of myself and this contact with married friends have convinced me that the value of celibacy lies beyond this practical sphere. Absence of sexual intimacy, just for the sake of pastoral activity, would be too high a price to pay. Rather it must be 'for the Kingdom' as the gospel says, in the sense of sharing in the heart of Christ. Only by entering that alternative love story, with its costs and its fulfilments, can one be liberated to care for people. Perhaps, therefore, celibacy should not be linked to priesthood as an obligation. But that is not the issue here. Our theme is how faith needs travelling together of various kinds, regardless of whether people are married or celibate. Especially today, faith without community seems a contradiction, an unnecessary handicap to our hopes.

VARIETY OF COMMUNITY

There are of course many other examples of the power of community in fostering faith. I think of the attraction of Taizé, the ecumenical monastery in the south of France, where thousands of secularized young people converge each summer to find spiritual nourishment and the experience of community. They share their hopes, and support one another in all sorts of ways from dish-washing to silence.

Above all they learn that life need not be such an egoist
prison, and that the cries of the world in need require them
to build themselves into living communities.

I was blessed to see yet another face of community in
Latin America. It is the secret of that continent, and of its
liberation spirituality, that its people have discovered a joy
in communities built from below. On any given evening one
can know that thousands of people are gathering in groups
of faith – centred on the Bible – where they listen to their
realities and discern their way of life. From just sitting in on
some of these gatherings, I learned that justice must begin
with such basics as water supplies or the collection of rubbish; for where the poor have been deprived in these ordinary needs, the communities of faith struggle to bring about
change in the spirit of the gospel. It was one of the joys of
my stay in Latin America to experience Sunday Mass within
alive communities of poor people. They took their time and
were not shy to share in response to the Scriptures. They
welcomed the stranger and were generous to any in need.
They sang with energy and prayed with devotion. Most of
all they communicated a confidence in their own kind of
Church; that was where their strength lay, where their hopes
were rooted, where their faith in God found central
expression.

Finally, what of my own experience of living as a religious
in community for nearly thirty years? Jesuits are not known
for community. We put less stress on it than some other
religious families. Even from the historical fact, so strange
at the time of our foundation, that we do not pray the
breviary in common, a certain individualism can become the
norm. But for me, community has come to be more and
more important with the years, especially as I have lived
mainly in small communities with students in formation.
Here there has been considerable interaction and mutual
support – from sharing the cooking to a commitment to

prayerful listening to what makes each person 'tick', from being there for each other in the dull everyday to more difficult facing of tensions among us. Probably my happiest experience has been to find myself surprisingly cared for: people challenged me over my excessive tiredness; they listened to struggles and supported me in all sorts of ways; they offered a friendship that never invaded, and an encouragement for my gifts that never forgot to tease my silly obsessions. For me another important experience of religious community has to do with 'obedience'; it has been good to know that decisions reached by 'superiors' were rooted in a care for me and for others, and in a prayerful search for what is best. It was consoling to be part of that process and to be listened to in a genuine way.

Strange to say, perhaps my deepest experiences of Jesuit community have been of forgiveness, where fellow-Jesuits accepted me in my difficult moods and thereby mirrored to me the compassion of God. It could be something as simple as being able to express anger enjoyably and without guilt, because the others took my feelings on board as a natural part of me. Let me recall one little incident of acceptance that I am grateful for: I was worried because one week I could not manage to take my turn in the cooking rota. When I mentioned this at our community meeting, the others attacked me, in friendly fashion, saying, 'Do you think we suspect you of shirking the work when you could do it? Aren't you out there doing something that we all think is worthwhile? This is a community, isn't it?' Rather like those Latin-American basic communities being at their best when bringing the vision of the Kingdom down into such everyday issues as water supplies, so religious community was at its best as 'friends in the Lord' who could tackle daily things in a gospel spirit.

Just as I was writing this chapter, I had a visit from an old friend of mine (not a Jesuit), who is about to leave for

some years in Africa. He is someone who reads and thinks
a lot, and who writes poetry from time to time. Since I am
moving to Rome, it may be years before we see one another
again. With that sense of farewell I found myself saying to
him: 'I hope you find friends there who can meet you in
your depths. More than that, I hope you can find others
who might share a project, a vision, a search of some kind.
Like the Magi.' Perhaps that is the difference between the
need for friendship and the need for community. Community is bigger, not only in numbers but because it builds
on a shared meaning and a shared goal. In this sense being
a Christian is to belong with others, and the rediscovery of
community – in exciting variety – is one of the truly consoling
signs of faith today.

The Herod Plot

I have sometimes tested the memory of people about the Magi story, inviting them to recall whatever details they could. Most people seemed to remember the star and the gifts but they often needed some prompting before mentioning what gets relatively a lot of space in St Matthew. 'Does this story have a villain?', I would ask. And only then would the Herod sub-plot come back to them.

It is striking that each of the Infancy stories in the gospel contains some note of hostility or conflict. The Annunciation at first causes Mary to be 'deeply disturbed'. Her Magnificat hymn of praise is also a prophecy against the rich and powerful. Months later the inn is shut against a pregnant woman. Later still Simeon at the very moment of his joyful recognition of the Messiah adds that Jesus will be 'rejected' and that Mary's soul will be pierced by a sword.

Thus these stories, which most of us encounter as children, have an adult edge to them as well. The entry of Christ into history entails division and opposition. There are those who receive him – like the shepherds and Simeon and Anna and the Magi – and those who close the door on him or even try to kill him – like Herod.

His main reason for wanting to be rid of Jesus was that he could not tolerate another king. It is a tale of two kinds of kingship. It is also a story of pretence, where

*the powerful one appears to be religious in order to
control the situation. 'When you have found him, let me
know, so that I too may go and do him homage.'*

*Where is Herod now? Surely alive and well and living
in our many systems of oppression, assuming various
disguises to continue his old deceptions in new ways.*

THE WORLDS OF CLARE AND ELISEO

'Are we all sucked into it, sooner or later, this rat-race? Is
there any hope of escaping its clutches?' I remember a sunny
afternoon in a London park when Clare poured out her
reactions to the strange world around her. She was spending
the summer as a trainee social worker and running into
plenty of 'reality'. In many ways she had foreseen those
tough realities and was ready for them – the desperation of
a single mother, alone with an infant and unable to find
friends; the suicidal depression of an ex-prisoner; the tensions of having to take a child away from two drug-addict
parents; the demanding old man who reported her 'bad
manners' to the office. To live with these situations day by
day was far from easy but something else was disturbing
Clare. Was it a sense of impotence before the accumulation
of problems in this city? Was it the contrast between this
underside of society and the other London, the smooth
wealth on display in the City and the West End? Was it the
seemingly cold professionalism that she noticed in older
social workers, as if they had to harden themselves to cope
with it all? All these things pressed in on Clare, but the key
to her unrest lay elsewhere. 'It's as if something sick is in
control – a kind of uncaring saturates this place. But there
must be something else, mustn't there? Where can God be
in all this?'

Faced with Clare's questions, on that sunny afternoon,
my temptation was to be too positive too quickly. It would

have been easy to say – and not untrue – that God was there
in the care that she was bringing to people. But her question
stemmed from a wider sense of trouble; she had glimpsed,
as it were, a system of egoism enthroned in this city, something that was larger than any of the victims whom she
visited in her work. This system, like a cynical Herod, was
able to shrug off any band-aid gestures of individual kindness: 'What harm are these do-gooders, as long as I run the
show?' Out of her personal experience, Clare was sensing
the futility of any merely personal responses if Herod continues to rule the kingdom.

Over against this memory of London, I want to set a
contrasting response from Paraguay. Once again it concerns
a young person of social conscience and high ideals. But in
Latin America the Herod-situation is different, and perhaps
it is easier to see one's way in a world of more obvious
oppression. Eliseo was a seminarian whom I got to know in
Asuncion in 1987, while General Stroessner was still dictator
(as he had been since 1954). Together with his fellow-stud-
ents Eliseo planned a special Stations of the Cross for the
Monday of Holy Week, which was to entail a procession in
the streets near the national seminary. Nothing could be
more normal for Latin America. But the students announced
that this commemoration of the Passion of Christ would be
in solidarity with peasant leaders evicted from their land and
imprisoned without trial. These men had been agitating for
land reform in a country where a small minority of the rich
holds nearly all the best land. Clearly, such a protest was
liable to bring down the wrath of the authorities. Besides it
was part of a history of tension between Church and regime
over justice for Paraguay's many impoverished farmers. Less
than a year before, when some peasants had been killed,
the bishops took the unprecedented step of calling out all
the priests and religious in the capital for a silent procession
carrying the Virgin of Ka'akupe. The police were powerless

to intervene, because although they might easily attack Church leaders, it would be unthinkable to insult Paraguay's most famous statue. Possibly in response to this challenge, General Stroessner's Christmas message for 1986 stressed the need to distinguish between 'good' and 'bad' priests. Good priests were those who served the spiritual needs of people, but bad priests used religion to interfere with society, disturbing the people with leftist notions of justice, and being disobedient to the Pope. (It is worth remarking that the same Pope on his visit to Paraguay in May 1988 proved himself to be a 'bad priest': his strong speeches on human rights were an acute embarrassment to Stroessner and may have helped towards the ousting of the dictator several months later.)

I mention all this to give some background for the story of Eliseo; his world of social conflict and of religious culture would differ enormously from that confronted by Clare in London. His response to his situation also had a quite different tone to Clare's: where she felt confused, isolated, and burdened by a sense of helplessness, Eliseo was confidently and happily rooted in a community of struggle larger than himself. As part of a Christian community he took part in that gesture of solidarity with the prisoners.

PERSECUTED IN THE CAUSE OF RIGHT

On the Monday afternoon in question, the procession of students and staff of the seminary got less than fifty yards outside the gates when it was attacked by police in riot gear. The peasant-made bare cross was broken, throwing its crown of thorns to the ground. Some thirty of the students were injured, two fairly seriously. Later that same day, Eliseo told me that as the batons fell on him, his pain gave way to anger: he wanted to scream out insults at the police. Then across his mind flashed a scene from the film *Gandhi* where the central figure stood with dignity as police rods crashed down on him, and Eliseo found himself thinking, 'If he could do it for his people, I can do it for mine and for Christ'. At that moment he sensed great peace in himself, in spite of the pain of the blows. The group had been beaten back behind the gates of the seminary. In the scuffles one of the police had lost his helmet and it now lay beside Eliseo. He could easily have kept it as a battle trophy but another spirit was at work. The Stations continued within the seminary grounds, with the police lined up only yards away at the entrance. As the prayers ended, Eliseo went forward to return the helmet to its owner, the only one without a helmet. It was roughly received, without even a word of thanks.

What for that policeman was an incomprehensible gesture sums up the spirit that moves many Latin American Christians in face of their many Herods. On that continent it is still possible to confront Herod in a gospel spirit and to hope to win. It is possible to have a sense of history in its slow making. By contrast the richer worlds of the West and the North seem spiritually stagnant, and ruled by a hidden and more dehumanizing Herod. It is harder for Clare to hope to make a difference than for Eliseo. In his world faith is more communally alive; in hers it has become a largely private affair – which gives Herod a more subtle victory and a more dangerous control. Where a merely personalist model of faith predominates, the Christian project of the Kingdom is cramped as in a straitjacket.

MOANING VS. CRITIQUE

In other parts of this book new hope is voiced, even for the more secularized and wealthy parts of our planet. But before Clare could set out on that more positive search, there is a job of negative discernment to be done. As Thomas Hardy once wrote, 'If way to the better there be, it entails a full look at the worst'. This task of seeing through the nonsense that surrounds us need not be a depressing business – in fact the contrary. What is depressing is to be a confused victim of forces that you never recognize. What is liberating is to grasp the nettle of critique as opposed to merely moaning. Moaning means simply complaining about 'this evil world'. But critique means taking a hard and discerning look at the ways our so-called 'common sense' is shaped. It means identifying the pressures that hold sway in our world. It means learning that the message of King Herod, the one in power, is not to be trusted. He is an arch deceiver, whose message seems attractive, friendly, interested in finding the baby king. But in fact he is plotting murder. Only when we see Herod clearly for what he is, can we hope to find our true way home.

Putting this more personally, my visits to Latin America confirmed a hunch that had been with me for some years – that many of my assumptions about faith were seriously distorted by my upbringing. It was like that moment in St Paul where he vehemently looks back on his formation in the law as 'rubbish', as something that damaged him until he found the fuller vision of Christ (Philippians 3:8). As a child I had no suspicions about the system surrounding me. Even later as a student, I lived within a set of assumptions about reality, without realizing that they were shaped in one narrow way of seeing the world. By the time I began to emerge from such 'ideological innocence', I had been well and truly moulded by a blinkered system. I can sum it up by saying that I was trained in passivity, privacy, and peace. Passivity meant that authority was always right; indeed you would be punished if you questioned it in any way. It also meant that change was evil, and that people who wanted to upset the *status quo* were rebelling against God. The message I received – from nobody in particular but as a global impression – was that the established way of life was the divine order of things. God had blessed those who were comfortable and they should be grateful, while those who were poor should carry their cross with resignation.

LOPSIDED UPBRINGING

The other distortion I received – at least I have now come to see it as a distortion – was the assumption that what went on inside my consciousness was crucially important, indeed the axis of my life. This is what I mean by privacy. It was a message that came to me from many quarters. It was dominant in the approaches to literature that I was educated into. Most of what I was taught about prayer – from primary school up to and including early Jesuit formation – implied that this separate inner self was the key to Christian living. It was not utterly untrue, but it now seems a dangerously lopsided view. But then modern culture is lopsided in many ways: in what it thinks of as 'objective' truth, in its despising of the feminine, in its destruction of community and the environment, and so on. It all adds up to a widespread isolation and alienation in Western society, and one which became easier for me to discern from the distance of Latin America.

The third falsity concerned peace. It was as if Christianity meant peace at any price. There was no place for anger or conflict. But in Latin America – as in the case of Eliseo – conflict is inevitable. When I re-read the gospels there, I began to see that Jesus found himself in continual conflict with the dehumanizing face of religion; ultimately it was a confrontation that would lead to his being killed. Previously I had often pondered and prayed the scene in Mark's Gospel where Jesus heals the man with the withered hand. I zoomed in on the healing of the individual and remained blind to the fact that the episode is mainly about conflict. We are

told that 'they were watching him' to see if he would dare
heal on the sabbath day. Indeed Jesus turns the scene
around, away from the victim and puts the authorities on
the spot, asking them a probing and ironic question: 'Is it
permitted on the Sabbath day to do good?' Are they here
to create or to destroy? We are told that their sitting on the
fence in silence angered him, and the scene ends with them
'discussing how to destroy him'. This simple scene is a perfect example of the 'aspect blindness' (a phrase from Witt-
genstein) that I picked up from my background and formation. I tended to see the incident in purely personal terms,
as a moment of healing; I ignored the fact that most of the
sentences describe tension. So it gives a whole new tone to
faith to realize the extent to which it can mean conflict with
the system – with the many ways in which Herod imposes
passivity, privacy, and a false kind of peace.

If this is true, then Herod rules today largely through the
unconscious assumptions all around us. Even though he pays
lip-service to religion, it is only to a religion that stays in
the sacristy or that serves a certain 'feeling good' by individuals. The net result is that Christianity is robbed of its
real power to change history. Instead it becomes cramped
into frozen forms of piety and into unconscious complicity
with Herod's plans. His anti-kingdom can take many forms:
it ranges from suffocating silliness to the injustices of our
divided planet. The Roman emperors provided bread and
circuses to keep the masses down; perhaps the modern
emperor has his Colosseum in the corner, in the shape of
television and video. It is like a plot to kidnap people's
imagination within the trivial and to brain-wash them into
unquestioning. No soldiers go forth with swords, but inno-
cents of all ages are lulled into stupor, so that the other
King is simply marginalized. Perhaps *the* enemy to faith
today is no longer a militant atheism but a Herod deceptively
pleasant, as was that gospel figure. The dominant culture of

the West does not attack faith openly: it just undermines it with other images and other priorities.

EXPOSING HEROD IN COMEDY

To end this section, I would like to draw on an intriguing exposure of Herod's deceptions in a recent film: Woody Allen's *Crimes and Misdemeanours* blends comedy and seriousness with exceptional success and manages to show how faith gets cornered in today's culture. On the surface it is about getting away with murder, literally, but it is also a study of how conscience is stifled in the 'real world'. The central figure is an eye specialist called Judah Rosenthal, who is trying to end an affair without his wife finding out. But from this banal material Allen constructs a drama of two ways of seeing the world. Judah is caught between the Jewish wisdom of his childhood, where God sees everything and therefore existence had moral stability, and the 'anything goes' ethic of Jack, his brother with underworld connections. One of his patients is a youngish rabbi called Ben who, symbolically, is going blind, and who mouths kindly but bland generalities at him: he should rekindle his faith and ask his wife's foregiveness, 'for without law all is darkness'.

The real enemy of such old morality and the king of this society is Lester, Ben's brother and a pompous television producer, famous for junk comedies; he suppresses an unfavourable documentary on his life and work, directed by Cliff, the Woody Allen character – who is as usual a lonely and worried searcher in this tough New York. The one impressive figure of wisdom is Professor Louis Levy, whom we only see on video speaking of how 'we define ourselves by our choices'; but in a shattering moment Cliff learns that this guru has committed suicide. In this playground of images all messages are unstable and all meanings fragile.

Thus, in spite of its many hilarious moments, *Crimes and Misdemeanours* is a serious exploration of what we have been describing as Herod's kingdom of deception. It is significant that at the end Judah has transformed his guilt into a television script that he outlines, somewhat tipsily, to Cliff at a wedding, and which ends: 'His life is completely back to normal, back to his protected world of wealth and privilege.'

Perhaps this film disturbs its audiences even more in its manner than in its content. It is not simply that the plot echoes the Herod strand of the Magi story; its mode of communication is a modern version of the 'dream' in that gospel narrative. In its impact on its viewers this film sounds a note of warning. If it undermines complacencies and prods consciences, it does so on the level of images rather than of ideas. This is the level of dreaming (about which more will be said in a later chapter). We are touching here on one of the roles for art within contemporary culture: it can alert the imagination to the falsities. It can, like the dream, serve as a warning system against sickness. It can mock the kingdom of Herod and leave people with a healthy suspicion about so-called normality and its charms. Although *Crimes and Misdemeanours* shows religion as ritualistic and out of touch, there is no doubt that its sympathies lie more with the ancient wisdom of faith than with the avoidance of guilt, the flouting of law, and the empire of triviality that triumphs in this world where 'God is a luxury I cannot afford'.

The House: Problems of Church

At the climax of the Magi's adventure is the moment of their discovery of Jesus. The star comes back to guide them after their interview with Herod, and it stops over the place that is the goal of their long journey.

Here St Matthew uses a little phrase that might seem insignificant and yet surely belongs with the symbolic vocabulary so frequent in the gospels. We are told that 'entering the house', they saw the child with Mary his mother. It is common knowledge that Matthew is the evangelist of the church, in the sense that he, more than the others, stresses the community of believers.

So 'house' in this text may suggest the special place that is church. It can also evoke all the spaces and places where God is encountered. Here it leads us to ponder the positives and negatives of church as experienced in today's world.

A PROBLEM INSTITUTION

It seems more honest to begin with the negatives. Over the years with students I have heard plenty of them. Some people might say that this reflects my Irish background; but while I have no doubt that the Church has a stronger presence in people's lives in Ireland than in many other countries, I am convinced that the key difficulties encountered over Church here are no different than elsewhere.

I recall one student called Cormac whom I knew quite well through his university years but who only after he graduated got to the point of voicing his religious blockages to me. Then one day he said that he wanted to pose a really big question to me, and he made quite a song and dance about coming to the point, saying that he was afraid he might offend me. What he came out with was: if Jesus came back now, do you not think the Church would do what the religious establishment did then – reject him and get rid of him? When I asked him to fill me in on the background of his question, he went back to his education in a Catholic secondary school and described how he came to see that institution as involved in a 'dishonest contradiction'. The school prided itself on challenging its pupils in matters of religion, and in particular on exposing them to issues of justice and injustice. But for Cormac the real curriculum was one of cut-throat competition in all fields – academic, athletic, and social. One episode in particular had soured his vision. Cormac was a talented sportsman and a key figure in the football team if the school were to win the cup that year. This also made him a popular figure in the school, someone who got a lot of attention from both staff and pupils. It happened that he injured himself badly at an early stage of the year and had to rest. So far so good. But the priest in charge of the team began to put pressure on him to return to training earlier than seemed right and Cormac resisted. It blew up into a quarrel, and the result was that Cormac decided to withdraw from the team entirely. Suddenly all the positive appreciation from the staff, religious and lay, dropped away and Cormac began to ask himself what were the real values of this Catholic school: care for people (as was always claimed officially) or a ruthless idolatry of competition (as he now experienced)?

This episode gave birth to a certain suspicion, which broadened into a doubt about all religious institutions. The

Church seemed another contradiction, officially standing for God's love, but in fact sucked into the worldly games and contaminated by them. Cormac admitted that it was rare for him to voice this root of his disenchantment. He usually contented himself with expressing the common criticisms of Church – about an empty atmosphere at Mass, about the paternalism of priests, about a predictable narrowness in church attitudes. But his main accusation went deeper than these dissatisfactions: he detected a fundamental falsity in the Church, a pretence of being spiritual and caring but a reality of being caught up in a pursuit of power and possessiveness.

CHURCH AS HUMAN

When I heard out Cormac's questioning to the full, I found it frightening in ways. It was his individual version of what Dostoevsky so terrifyingly portrayed in his parable of the Grand Inquisitor – a manipulating manager of people's religious needs who did not want any Christ to 'disturb' his neatly functioning institution. Cormac's query was far from merely intellectual; he was asking me how I could stay as a priest within what he viewed as a dishonest institution. What could I say to him in response? First of all, a 'yes' to what is true in his criticism of Church: it can become a place of falsity and of twistedness. Yes, the Church in its human dimension is just that – human, and therefore, like me or Cormac, capable of goodness or of falling very short of what we are meant to be. But in case this admission of guilt seem too glib, I admit that the Church gives much more scandal when it falls short than does some institution that does not take its stand on such sacred ground. Perhaps that is what lies behind anger of many a Cormac, that they seek and expect a place of visibly lived Christianity – of care and compassion, of community and contemplation. Precisely because they are disappointed in these gospel-hopes, they sense a greater let-down than with institutions like universities or governments that also fall short of their ideals. The hopes of the Cormacs whom I have known are often grounded in genuinely Christian intuitions.

Although I could recognize and agree with many of his causes of complaint, there remained major differences between my response and his. How could I stay within this flawed Church? I had a different sense of things and for two reasons; one was fairly predictable, the other more surprising. The predictable one related to the generation or culture gap between us. Unlike Cormac, who is a child of the seventies, I grew up in a way that gave me stronger roots in Catholicism, through happy experiences of childhood religion, and through inheriting a certain loyalty to the Church. The strength of those spiritual memories means that I can tolerate the warts of church life because I sense a wider wisdom there. Of course I want the warts removed, or at least reduced, but in practice I don't ever expect an ideal Church. I am less shocked than Cormac by the Church of sinners that is, alas, our human reality.

Which brings me to the surprising reason: could it be that Cormac remains romantic in his critique because he is too innocent about sin? That is what I found myself saying to him. I knew, of course, that the very word would be strange to him, that he could be allergic to it from childhood. Exactly my point. If his only view of sin came from childhood, then his needle was stuck in this respect. The child's model of wrongdoing as breaking the rules would not fit the larger scandals of sin in our world, including the sin of hypocrisy that he discerned within the Church.

INNOCENT ABOUT SIN?

This is a big topic and a difficult one, and I am in danger of being misunderstood. It could sound like avoiding his accusation by changing the agenda: 'The Church seems corrupt to me'; 'Ah, but your trouble is that you have no sense of sin'. That could come across as a false shifting of the argument. Instead, I intend it as taking his accusation of dishonesty to its ultimate level of seriousness, which in religious language is called sin.

How on earth are we to make sense of 'sin' today? for Cormac, or indeed for anyone who grows out of the obedience model of reality? Already, in thinking about Herod we have seen something of the powerful forces of deception and evil at work in our world. But the key difference between evil and sin is that sin implies some personal responsibility. To speak of a Church of sinners is to acknowledge something that is not at some comfortable distance from us, like a civil war in a distant land. So what is this thing called 'sin'?

Let me answer with a true story. Some months ago I was asked to say the twelve o'clock Mass in Ballymun, where I have lived for three years. In this area which has some of the highest levels of unemployment in Ireland, only a small proportion of people attend church. But those who do bring something special and vibrant. Behind the success of the twelve o'clock Mass lies a group of lay people, who meet the previous Monday evening to prepare the liturgy; and the priest who is to celebrate sits in on this meeting. On this particular Monday in Lent the theme was sin, which at first seemed a gloomy topic. At one point one of the women said, almost in jest, 'Could you possibly make sin seem happy? After all the gospel is meant to be good news.' It seemed a tall order, but we took it as our discussion point. Remembering something from Scripture studies years ago,

I remarked that the Greek word for sin in the gospels comes from archery and actually means 'missing the mark'. This proved to be the spark that our group imagination needed. One man offered to make a big drawing of a target of circles with an arrow falling short, and this would hang in front of the altar. Another woman suggested that in my homily I should not mention the word sin until the very end, that I should talk about us missing-the-mark, God's target being lives of love. And so it became the Sunday when *we* (because it was plural) managed to communicate a happy sense of sin.

CHURCH: WARTS AND WISDOM

To return to the central point, and to my response to Cormac, it is as naive to expect the Church to show no signs of sin, as it would be to expect oneself to be always a paragon of shining goodness, someone who never misses the mark. I fear that such a dismissal of the Church remains superficial until it is forced to confront the struggle of good and evil in every human heart. Even though some of the language used about Church seems to imply an ideal state of sanctity, that is not the human reality of its members, whether they are in authority or in the pews or like Cormac, on the margins. Although it may be hard to forgive the warts of the Church, it is no surprise to find my own flawed humanity mirrored even in the institution that is meant to serve Christ in this world.

Finally, I want to offer Cormac a double message, even a seemingly contradictory one. You have had too much church, I would say to him, so much so that it has become a block from growth into faith in Christ – so forget the Church for the moment *if* it helps you to enter on a deeper journey of religious meaning. But, I would equally insist, in the long run you will get lost without the Church; without the support of a community and of a tradition, where will you find friends for your road? Life is far too short to waste in lonely questioning. Without some companionship, such as the Church at its best can give, you could be condemned to a private search that never finds a language of life with others. It is the isolated fate of many within our western culture today. So my final answer to Cormac's question would be: I remain within the Church for many reasons, but perhaps mainly because I find goodness and strength and even sanctity here. Ultimately I find God. And all this out-weighs the sad failures of vision, even though it can never condone them. It was Jesus himself who told a parable about the Kingdom as a field of wheat where weeds grew as well; when the workers are shocked by the presence of weeds and want to pull them up, the wise owner tells them that to do so would damage the wheat, and that they should wait until the harvest. The parable points to the mixture of good and evil in any human field. Cormac's shock, like that of the workers, was in many ways justified, but a larger horizon, like the owner's, would lead to a more compassionate response.

So for me the Church is the community that – in spite of human failings – guards the memory of Christ for each new moment of history. Our hearts need reminding of him. Our imaginations needs re-nourishing with him. Our choices need re-challenging by him. Our spirits need renewal in him. And our lives need companionship in following him. The Church exists to guide and serve that long adventure of living out the vision that he called the Kingdom. Chesterton once remarked that the Church 'is the one thing that saves a person from the degrading servitude of being a child of one's own time'. And, I would add, from believing one's own little self to be the only measure of meaning.

Falling to their Knees: Prayer

At the heart of the Magi story is the moment of adoration. It is, we are told, a physical act of reverence that these sages offer to the infant Jesus. It expresses something of wonder and awe before the presence of God in this child.

Traditionally this moment is celebrated in the feast called Epiphany, and the focus is on the moment of recognition of God in human form. Artists and poets have been fascinated with this scene, often seeing it as a revolution in wisdom; the Magi thought they were bringing gifts to some new human king, but instead found themselves receiving a glimpse of God, with the flow of gifts reversed.

This core moment in the story evokes the many languages of prayer. At the centre of every religion is some meeting with God. At the centre of Christianity is an encounter with God through Jesus.

How can this meeting happen today? More simply how can we arrive at the threshold of prayer? And what is it like to cross that threshold into some experience of the presence of God?

AGNOSTICS CAN PRAY

That heading is not intended just to catch the attention; it has its origins in experience with unbelievers. I want to recount one in some detail to show that a spiritual life is possible for everyone, independent of religious faith or Church belonging. It also seems right to approach the question of prayer from below, as it were, as a human adventure in awareness first of all – even though it is more than that, as we shall see later.

I want to tell the story of Derek, a politically alert young man who had an unusual religious background for Ireland in that his parents were agnostic and he had been brought up without any religious formation. The school he attended was Catholic and he did quite well in 'religious knowledge' without it ever becoming a reality for him. He learned some of the content of faith, and some stories of the Bible, without it being more than an interesting tale. But Derek was artistic in temperament, especially gifted in music and liked to express himself in poetry. This was what brought him into personal contact with me for the first time: from being in class with me, he wanted to ask my opinion on some poems he had written. They explored his own memories and feelings in a very honest way. Many of them seemed to be about hurts in relationships and about smoldering resentments. We moved from talking about the texts to talking about the underlying experiences, which in fact centred on his elder brother. Derek had been close to him when they were younger but with his brother's marriage a painful gap seemed to come between them. He was particularly hurt by the fact that whenever they planned some occasion together – like an outing, a game of tennis, even a meal at his brother's house – it was nearly always cancelled at the last moment by his brother. This led Derek to wonder whether his sister-in-law disliked him, or was not at ease with him, but his own feelings were wounded and confused. At one point in telling me all this Derek remarked – almost flippantly – 'If I were a Christian, you could tell me to pray for the grace of forgiveness'. 'Perhaps you can still pray in your own way, even as an unbeliever', I replied, equally playfully and yet serious. 'Even without God?' 'Why not? Let's call it meditation.'

And so it began – our plan to meet together over a few weeks for guided meditation. The first step was to learn some skills of stillness and to practise them each day. The exercise that seemed to help Derek most was one that is called *vipassana* in the East; this involves letting the awareness gather round all the various physical sensations of the skin – literally from top to toe. One simply moves the focus of one's awareness, like radar, down all the body's surfaces, and back up again. If one does this several times, slowly and gradually banishing other distracting drains on one's attention, it is normal to discover many, varied sensations of which one is not usually conscious. The object of the exercise is to provide an anchor of stillness, a rudder for the unruly attention. Once the self is anchored through this noticing of the senses (and this may easily take ten or fifteen minutes) then the person can listen to the emotions or memories that come from the depths of themselves. This is exactly what happened for Derek. He found a place and a time each day to practise this form of focusing for at least ten minutes and then listen to his feelings. I suggested that he get in touch with his feelings of gratitude for just being alive and for his brother in particular. He came back after a few days of this to report that he found it remarkably easy and fruitful. The simple method of creating quiet helped him to relax and he found that his older feelings of anger and resentment were less dominant. He was delighted to be able to recognize more positive emotions within himself and to enjoy them.

INNER JOURNEY MINUS GOD

'But would you call this prayer?' Derek asked me with some doubt in his voice. If prayer means some deliberate reaching out to God, I told him, perhaps it's not prayer strictly speaking. But put it the other way round. Suppose there is a God. The only God worth believing in would want to reach out to you, and whether or not you recognize that is secondary. When you learn to listen to your deepest self, perhaps you are entering one of the places where God is reaching out to you in shy silence. And that may be the only kind of prayer you are capable of for the moment. But trust your experience. Don't mind about the interpretation of it for now. It is possible that this experience is just secular even if spiritual in a human way; it is also possible that it is a meeting of your spirit and the Spirit of God. Enjoy the experience and gather the fruits. Explanations can wait.

So Derek the self-styled atheist or agnostic continued on his path of meditation. Every few days he came to reflect on his progress, and with some suggestions from me he found himself realizing much more of a sense of wonder and trust within himself than he had been aware of for a long time. 'Since when?' I asked. 'Probably since childhood', he replied. Exactly. Derek was getting in touch with the trusting child within him, with that deeper experience of himself that had recently been eclipsed in temporary fashion by the hurts and disappointments caused by his brother. Once he was in touch with this older base of joy and aliveness, with his true self, it was safe to confront the more negative experiences. To have started with them directly would not have helped.

Thus after about ten days of daily quiet times, when Derek was able to relax into the reality of being grateful for his life, I suggested that he continue with the entrance exercise of physical focusing but gently to face also the less happy feelings and memories. As a headline for this shift of wavelength, I gave Derek a scene from the gospel to ponder, from chapter five of Luke. It tells of Jesus borrowing Peter's boat to speak to the crowds. Afterwards as if to thank him for the use of the boat, Jesus invites Peter to move to deep

waters and to let down his nets. Peter responds with a
mixture of failure and trust: 'We worked hard all night long
and caught nothing, but if you say so, I will pay out the
nets.' When he does this, the nets fill to bursting point and
at the sight of this Peter, we are told, 'fell at the knees of
Jesus saying, "Leave me, I am a sinful man" '. This scene
on its own would be rich enough for many a meditation,
and of a kind that Derek could enter on without any faith
dimension of the usual kind. It is a story of emptiness
(nothing all night), of trust (he tries again because Jesus
invites him), of fullness and amazement (the huge catch)
and then of unworthiness (a sinful man). Derek could easily
identify with the first three emotions – as echoing his own
experiences of failure, of confidence in a friend, and of
aliveness or gratitude. But why the sense of unworthiness
and why *then*? Would not a more normal reaction be to
thank Jesus or, in more traditional religious language, to
'praise the Lord'?

UNWORTHINESS WITHOUT GUILT

I had another story up my sleeve, so to speak, one that
stemmed from an extraordinary coincidence. Some years
previously another student had sat in exactly the same chair
as Derek and had a similar period of guided prayer – except
that in his case it was prayer rooted in Christian faith. His
name was Peter and he ran into a similar puzzlement over
the reaction of his namesake at this point in the gospel. But
as it happened he had a most unusual breakthrough into a
solution. He was celebrating his twenty-first birthday during
the university term and, being far from his family, decided
to invite a wide circle of student friends to gather in a pub,
at least to begin the night. They all agreed. However as the
day approached, more and more of them cried off, explaining that they couldn't make it that evening. Peter ended up

with only four, and although disappointed, managed to hide his hurt. They went to the pub together, but then one of the girls suggested it would be more pleasant to move back to Peter's flat, perhaps buying something to eat on the way. Back they went to a major surprise! On opening the door, he found everyone he had invited and more, and the whole flat decorated. As he told me afterwards, he collapsed into a chair near the door as they all sang 'Happy Birthday' – and felt unworthy. At that strange moment he understood the other Peter, and why, when surrounded by giftedness, one realizes one's own poverty. Perhaps it is only when 'overwhelmed by miracle' (a phrase from Yeats) that it is safe to face one's shadow side.

All this is a long way of saying that for Derek to deal with his churned up resentments and other negative reactions, it was necessary first to ground himself in gratitude and in a sense of the goodness of life. And he could do all this at some depth of self-listening without explicit faith. He had the courage not to avoid those 'deep waters' and I had confidence that if he remained faithful to letting his net down daily into those waters, he would not be far from the Kingdom. Even though no huge conversions of faith occurred for Derek, he certainly discovered a spiritual wavelength within himself and arrived at new freedoms that he needed – as we shall see.

Armed with the gospel text as an anchor for his imagination, Derek was now ready to deal with his own anger, guilt, hurt and so on. As before, he was to create inner peace (the physical awareness exercise), next gather his sense of gratitude from the previous week (like the full net) and only then to pause deliberately on his more painful emotions, seeking to hear them and say goodbye to what might be unworthy in them. Approached in this spirit, the negatives could be purified of what might be unworthy of Derek himself (shallow or prejudiced reactions) or of others (being too quick to judge them harshly).

His second week of meditation proved more difficult in some ways, but ultimately it was fruitful as well. The difficulties arose from a certain resistance to the zones of pain, and as Derek discovered, from a fear that he would find himself exposed as equally to blame. But even though some day's efforts seemed to lead nowhere, he kept going, until on one particular day during the silence he discovered himself in tears. He had been thinking about his brother and about the gap that had opened up between them. Suddenly he was overwhelmed by a sense of sadness, as if his brother had died, and he realized that much of his resentment was in fact a kind of mourning over the loss of his brother in marriage. He had come in touch with his own vulnerability and loneliness, and it was easy enough now to forgive his brother and even, as was equally necessary, to forgive himself.

FROM HEALING TO CHOICE

When we met to reflect on the week, Derek had arrived at a clearer view of the pain that he had broached in our first conversation. He was able to own his responsibility in clinging to his angers. A certain honesty had opened a door to new freedom for him. He could now handle his relationship with his brother more serenely. Thus in a sense we had finished what we set out to do. Or had we? I asked Derek if he thought there were more areas to visit through this kind of daily meditation. Without any hesitation he replied, 'Yes, what am I to do with my life and why?'

It was as if clearing up the negatives was not enough. Now that they had been addressed, now that he was discovering a daily avenue into his own depths, the compass of his desire swung in a fresh direction – towards decision and

commitment, with an accompanying hunger for self-mean-
ing. He explained to me that he was left with a new but
happy dissatisfaction with himself. All the explorings of
these weeks had put him in touch with an inner self that he
had previously ignored. He looked back on the way he had
been living as a kind of helpless drifting, happy enough in
its own way but missing out on many possibilities. So at one
point he threw the question to me, 'Where do you think I
am in all this?' I found myself saying, 'You've found the
child in you; now you want to find the adult'. It was a little
too neat a summary, yet it had its truth. Up to now his inner
journey had enabled Derek to enter the realm of feelings –
of trust and wonder, and later of vulnerability and pain.
Now that he was able to embrace this 'child' dimension of
himself with both courage and compassion, it was only
natural to want to focus on owning his 'adult' future. Healing
of any kind usually opens the door to hope.

For the next week we agreed on a different strategy.
Derek would continue to use whatever skills of stillness
helped him to find a steady level of listening. But then
he would pause on people whom he admired in any way,
harvesting the memories of goodness that he had glimpsed
in others. It could involve famous spiritual leaders like
Gandhi or Martin Luther King or people in his own circle,
like his mother who had come through a major illness with
her usual serenity and humour. After letting his imagination
rest on whatever moved him in such figures of sanctity,
Derek was then to reflect and see what this called forth in
his own humanity. Although I did not tell him in advance,
my hope and aim in suggesting this was that he would
awaken and identify some of the desires of his heart, and
so find an answer to his own question.

It proved fruitful well beyond what I had expected. Derek
returned the following week with a different energy in his
voice. 'It's very simple,' he said, 'I want to lead a generous

life from now on.' He went on to describe how he found himself drawn in fantasy to hold a long conversation with – of all people – Jesus. He had tried out some other ideal people but gradually he discovered that his image of Jesus, even though vague in many ways, was a more powerful attraction for dialogue. Somewhere in his past he had encountered the saying 'Love one another as I have loved you' and this formed the hinge of their imaginary conversation. 'Don't get me wrong,' Derek warned me, 'I'm as agnostic as before about all the God stuff. Just because I was imagining Jesus doesn't mean I was "praying" as you might do. But it did seem to release my hopes and I know that I want to make a difference in this world. Like he did. That's something I think I can hang on to, even though I don't know what form it could take in practice.'

Listening to this surprising development, I felt a great reverence for the point at which Derek had now arrived. Part of me would have loved to steer him towards a more explicit Christian faith but another, wiser part of me felt that the journey into freedom he had experienced would surely bear fruit in the long term, and perhaps in the direction of faith. He was certainly more open than ever before – both to his own human call and to the depths discovered through his inner adventure. I decided to trust in the rhythm of the Spirit, who had been at work (at least as I saw it) during these weeks. To have made an option for 'a generous life', one that was inspired by the figure of Jesus, was sufficient fruit for the moment.

THE SUPPRESSED SPIRITUAL

Having decided to leave behind these fairly intense exercises in meditation, Derek and I found ourselves reflecting back on the whole experience. 'Do you think you have changed much?' I asked him. 'Yes and no', he replied, 'would be the truest answer. In one way I'm delighted with my discovery of a process of listening to reality. That's a major change. I never knew such a wavelength was possible for me. But the change I needed was not what I first thought. It wasn't simply a matter of sorting out my confused feelings about my brother. It was much more that I needed some rudder for my own existence as a whole. And you were able to provide one from the religious tradition. I imagine you would describe the entire thing in more spiritual language, would you?'

Yes, the inspiration behind my suggestions had come from the *Spiritual Exercises* of Ignatius of Loyola. From that famous text – and from my own repeated experience of its process – I had the conviction that 'graces' (or, in secular language, freedoms) usually came in a certain sequence. Thus I advised Derek not to face his more negative feelings until he had spent time getting in touch with a sense of wonder and gratitude. Later, when he had worked through the woundedness a bit, it was natural for him to open out his agenda of searching into options and choices. The three stages that he had experienced could be named as basic trust, followed by what the old spiritual tradition would term the purgative and illuminative ways, or in more contemporary language, get in touch, face the shadow, own your life. The sad thing is that in Herod's culture of chatter many people are kidnapped into scatteredness and never guess at these potentials that lie within their experience. What was special about Derek's 'spiritual exercises' is that his agnosticism proved no barrier to his travelling on a road of spiritual liberation influenced by the Christian tradition.

Finally, it is worth recording his own conclusions when he looked back later on his unusual journey. 'If this is spirituality,' he remarked, 'why is it such a closely guarded secret? Why is religion, as most people find it, so associated with boring rituals and cheap words? Even if I can't make sense of God, at least I can glimpse the depths of us where God might be lurking, waiting to be found. But most believers are deprived of this level of self-discovery. To me it seems as if religion is failing its own core vision.'

In his own way Derek was voicing a major critique of religion in practice, one that sounds with a special urgency today. To return to the images of the Magi story, where can people find a genuine 'house' experience today, where adoration is possible in a transformative and creative way? The hunger for the contemplative dimension of religion has never been more acute than in this era of sensate stimulation – all of which leads us to another example of a different explorer in that direction.

FROM LITERATURE TO SILENCE

It was after an evening class on George Eliot's *Middlemarch* that I first talked to Joanne. She approached me as I was going upstairs to my office, and surprised me by saying 'Thank you for a most spiritual lecture'. 'That's an unusual compliment', I replied, and so we ended up talking for an hour or so in my room – until the ten o'clock bell rang to clear the university for the night. By 'spiritual' she meant that the session had touched on some crucial issues: how to live without the old clarities about God, how to cope with the spiritual loneliness of any searcher nowadays, how to salvage some religiousness when formal religion fails to touch lives, how to find food for the transition from 'egoism' to 'sympathy', and how a woman can make any difference in the real world, or must she live in an 'unhistoric' life? (The words in quotes are those of George Eliot.)

So we spoke about literature as a long dialogue about basics, especially since the collapse of traditional religion in the last century. Many imaginative writers, whether believers or not, have been engaged in a search for ultimates and have formed, as it were, a conspiracy of spirituality. With negative energy they have promoted suspicion about the complacencies of their cultures; at the same time, and with a certain shyness, they have defended non-rationalist intuitions of truth. Not only was there George Eliot's quest for a substitute wisdom, an ethics of compassion in the absence of God. Think of how Lawrence passionately defends the God-flame within humanity. Then there is Aldous Huxley's conversion in mid-career from cynical satirist to explorer in search of mystical awareness. Or T. S. Eliot's similar emergence from a despairing poetry of fragments into one that seeks to evoke religious experience across the boundaries of religions. Or more recently, Saul Bellow's satire of the stifled soul in crowded cities, as he leads his central figures to liberation, to trusting their hearts' hunches, where 'the depths of the spirit are never overcrowded'. Or Patrick White, who seeks to awaken a sense of mystery and 'to give professed unbelievers glimpses of their own unprofessed religious factor'. Or Flannery O'Connor's assaults on the armour-plated pride of modernity, humbling her central figures into knowing their need for revelation. What about Yeats, or Forster? Or even Beckett, whose work centres on our comic inability to accept meaninglessness and who is obsessed with a religious-like hunger that will not die? And the list could go on.

In that first conversation with Joanne, as we wandered around this vast field, I found myself reaching for a quotation from T. S. Eliot; what he once remarked about Hawthorne and James could easily apply to this whole tradition of imagination in quest of meaning, that they displayed 'indifference to religious dogma and at the same time exceptional awareness of spiritual reality'. At this point Joanne turned the focus on me, asking if this latent spirituality was a justification for a priest to teach literature in a secular university. It was part of it, I replied, saying that I enjoyed the challenge of standing where worlds converge. But what about revelation and contemplation? Surely they were the foundations of any religion, countered Joanne. Were they not in effect banished by the secular ethos, and was that not a frustration for me? Yes, indeed, theology is forbidden in the university founded by Cardinal Newman, which must leave him spinning in his grave. And yes, in practice it is 'not on' for me to speak of explicitly religious horizons like Scripture and prayer. Except in private, when invited, as with Joanne now.

HOW DO YOU PRAY?

At first I had imagined her to be some variety of agnostic, perhaps a contemporary echo of George Eliot. How wrong I was! It gradually emerged that she had a profound commitment to an inner life, that she had explored Buddhism and the spiritual sides of Jung, and that she gave some regular time to daily silent meditation. What she was not sure of was her relationship to the Catholicism and Christianity of her upbringing. She had not rejected it but neither was it in the forefront of her spiritual life at present. Her key question to me, when she got to it, proved to be a curious one: how did I, as a Christian, pray and above all, did I trust the silence? Behind Joanne's inquiry, as it turned out, was a sense that Christianity seemed less contemplative than eastern religions, that what most people found in Catholicism were rituals, rules and prayers (plural – like Our Fathers and Hail Marys), and therefore that silent meditation, such as she had discovered and developed, seemed discouraged or at least neglected.

Alas, what Joanne voiced is a common impression that is both true and false. It is true that many people never get the opportunity to acquaint themselves with the spiritual tradition of the West. But it is false that Catholicism lacks ways of contemplative wisdom. An encounter with mystery lies at the heart of Christianity; the definiteness of Christ as Incarnate God and the concreteness of his new command of love should in no way diminish the mystical core of Christian faith. All too often the pressures of the practical have relegated the spiritual to an optional extra, making it seem a specialization for religious rather the birthright of every believer; or allowing it to be taken up by the world of art and literature – as we were saying – with a richness frequently absent in official religion.

What could I say to Joanne about prayer? Her question was not about the theology of prayer but about my own experience of what she called 'silence'. In this sense she was putting me on the spot and looking for a personal answer. At the time, and in several subsequent meetings, I tried to meet her question, as well as to hear her own side of things. What I want to communicate here is something of what we discovered together, through our mutual efforts to dialogue about silence and the spirit.

DEFEATING THE MONKEYS

I admitted to Joanne that I am unsteadily faithful to a daily space of silence that I call prayer. I say unsteadily because it has often been sold short or performed without care, or just jettisoned under pressure. But usually it is there somehow and it is something very important to me. Without it I fear I would be even more stuck with a 'heart of stone' and less in touch with the 'heart of flesh' (Ezekiel 36:26). Over the years it has been a slowly changing adventure that is hard to put into words, but it has certainly moved from something more complex to something more simple. When I think back now on the complicated 'points' I used to make as a novice – heady ideas on the Scriptures, written at night for the morning's meditation – I feel a thousand miles from that older self. Gradually I grew to prefer silence and to think of it as the language of God. Not that it is always easy to rest in total quiet: the tree of self is full of jumpy monkeys, as a guru once said to me in India. Where Joanne and I found much common ground was in the area of skills for stillness, and how we need ways of centring the scattered self (somewhat as described in talking about Derek). I surprised Joanne by saying that I have no difficulty in praying, but hastened to add that I have huge difficulty getting myself to the threshold of prayer. Perhaps the secret lies in self-patience when the monkeys are jumpy and in having ways to tranquillize them. The problem is having the courage to create the stillness, but once that point is passed, prayer happens naturally.

In this respect, and on a practical level, I shared one piece of advice with Joanne. If those first few minutes are crucial as setting an inner atmosphere either of listening or of unease, then are there any practical helps that can steer that opening time? I think there are, and I call my formula 'roca' (the Spanish word for rock). Each letter stands for something that facilitates the possibility of deeper prayer. R stands for reverence, a fundamental requirement; if I remember to whom I reach out, then both physically and internally I will have an attitude of reverence. The story of the Magi in fact mentions both the outer and inner: falling down and adoring. O stands for offering, in the sense of promising the time and the effort to keep one's appointment, to be present from the heart. C stands for centring, for all that range of methods that can quieten the frivolous monkeys within. It is possible to take one's temperature very quickly, so to speak, and to know whether the conditions of silence are present or not. If quiet comes naturally, then forget about techniques of centring, but if it looks like one of those bad days, then time is well spent in laying the foundations of listening. Usually this means having the

humility to let *one* sense impression gather the straying
mind: repeating a phrase, listening to sounds, becoming
aware of the touch of one's hands, looking at the flame of
a candle, even voicing one's feelings aloud if circumstances
allow – these or many another simple anchor can, if patiently
attended to, work wonders for stillness. Finally, A stands
for asking, and here is where Joanne found herself resisting
the simplicity of my suggestions. She could follow me up to
this point but to stress asking seemed to her like 'old-
fashioned prayer of petition'. Is it ever old-fashioned? I
asked. Is it not rather at the heart of prayer to come before
God in need? Asking gives focus to desire, and prayer is
the language of desire. Ask for what? For the big things,
like peace, love, wisdom, and the Spirit.

AWARENESS OR RELATIONSHIP

Our disagreement over asking was the pointer to a more
basic difference. Joanne was not sure whether or not she
was praying to a personal God. For her it was easier to look
on meditation time as an awareness exercise, rather than to
think of herself as entering into any relationship with a God
beyond her. For me the awareness exercise was only a means
– often an essential means – to the contact with God which
was the aim of prayer. This was a significant difference of
emphasis and of interpretation (and one to which we would
return), but the ground of our dialogue remained; in Joanne's own words, it lay in the spiritual experience of silence.

With respect for her hesitations, I want, first of all, to
evoke this experience in words that do not stress the
relationship with God; later, we can bring in the explicitly
Christian sense of prayer. To immerse oneself in silence has
become a luxury within the rhythms of life today. To many
people it seems weird to set time aside for total quiet; to
me it seems weird not to. It is within such quiet space that

the heart tunes into a wavelength unreachable otherwise. It dares to exit from the everyday and to be rescued from the blinkers of the practical. It enters into the un-understandable. What seems like withdrawal opens out into deeper involvement with everything and everyone. From the horizon of silence, the heart can see through the small comforts and small concerns, the shoddy stuff that kidnaps us (Herod's plot again); but, nourished on silence the heart can expand into a compassion that both consoles and makes demands.

This kind of silence is a healing and strengthening space, a place where the daily dishonest gap between words and deeds is bridged. It is hard to describe what happens there except that the self moves from emptiness and the shame of its shadows into belonging. It moves from unworthy, fragile peace into costly and genuine peace. And this encounter with quiet has – and must have – its fruits in the ordinary: in some way, hard to pinpoint, this time of listening adjusts the heart's uncertain compass towards love. Without that acid test of giving and compassion, the whole thing could be self-concerned. Learning to love is the only worthy goal for all this silence. Indeed there is nothing special about silence – except that, as life goes on, it is often the best language of listening and learning. In the exposure of silence there is little room for dishonest games. Besides, it is our safest language for mystery and for God, well beyond the inadequacies of mere words.

SPECIFICS OF CHRISTIANITY

Something of all that and more must have happened to the Magi in their moment of adoration. Indeed that famous scene offers a perfect example of where Joanne could meet the contemplative note of Christianity: it unites the silent encounter with mystery central to all religions with the more personal presence of God in Jesus, specific to Christianity. All the great religions of the East specialize, so to speak, in avenues of searching for the divine, and are marvellously rich in scaffolding for silence. But Christianity has a different starting point and makes a more startling claim: it is not so much that we have to search for God (that is true but secondary), as that God has searched for us 'at many moments in the past and by many means' (the opening of the Letter to the Hebrews). But God's ultimate quest happens in Jesus, who has been sent to find us and to show us the way.

What might Joanne find or imagine in that Magi moment of adoration? Those wise travellers had come to bring gifts to a new king. Did they penetrate the identity of this particular King? The gospel does not say, but it lets us suppose that they did, even in some obscure faith without words. If so, they experienced a reversal, a change in the direction of their journey. Where they thought they were the gift-bringers, they now discover themselves to be the receivers of a much greater gift. In that prayer of adoration their hearts must have realized something of the revolution and revelation present before them: at the core of Christianity is a God who comes to us in our humanity. This reaching out by God is so simple and yet so radically different from anything found in eastern religions. It lifts our burden of lonely spiritual journeying. It promises a side-by-side companionship on the road from life into Life. Thus the centre of our silence is inhabited; it is no longer an absence but a presence, moreover a presence with a human face. Such a conversion from an abstract belief in God to a more personal faith in Jesus Christ is what should define a Christian, and yet it can be sadly rare even among church-goers.

A Christ-discovery of this kind changed the tone of Joanne's silence. Slowly and over months she continued her daily spiritual space but now she turned more to the Scriptures for nourishment. She kept her practice of quiet, but it now became a wordless encounter with a friend, a conversation of the heart beyond language. Sometimes of course she would use words, would ponder gospel scenes, but the key to her prayer was a resting in a new silence of presence. And then one day Joanne came to tell me of another discovery, one that she made herself with the help of some reading. 'Why', she asked me, 'did you not tell me about the Trinity?' 'I assumed you knew; and besides it seemed too complicated to go into.' But the opposite was true: the reality of Father, Son, and Spirit had become for Joanne a rich anchor for her prayer and her life. Previously of course she had known *about* the Trinity, in the sense of having heard of the doctrine. But she had never known its relevance for her. What she had now discovered, however, was that the three persons answered to three dimensions of her life.

THE TRINITY AS REAL

The Father is the God beyond us whom 'no one has ever seen' (John 1:18), and hence for Joanne the God of mystery, encountered in a prayer of silence. The Son, by contrast, showed us God as one like ourselves, one who struggled and loved, who said that as often as we 'did this to the least of these', we did it to him. For Joanne this other face of God is encountered mainly in the calls of others and in serving the hungers of our wounded world, as well as in the Scriptures, the sacraments, and prayer that speaks directly to Christ. The Spirit is God within our hearts, leading us towards love, helping us to recognize our gifts (1 Cor 2:12) and to set them free for others. This is the secret presence of God within every person, believer or unbeliever; and this Spirit aids our lostness in prayer and carries our longings 'in a way that could never be put into words' (Romans 8:26).

Joanne had hit upon her own sense of the Trinity and upon her own answer to our central question, Where is your

God? God is in silent mystery – the Father. God continues in all humanity – the Son. God dwells in every heart and conscience – the Spirit. This gave her an exciting new synthesis for prayer and faith. Gradually she moved from being committed to the vaguely spiritual to being committed to the Christian vision of the spiritual, and she lost nothing on the way. What had started as an interest in interiority had broadened out to become genuine prayer. What had begun as awareness exercises in stillness became both personal and interpersonal. At the outset Joanne's focus was on the adventure of the inner self; now she found herself drawn into finding her place within the bigger drama of this struggling world.

A footnote to this story of Joanne: I have never known an atheist who fully appreciated the Trinity. Perhaps the god that atheists refuse is the Lonely God in the Sky as often as not, and they simply do not know the Trinity except as a piece of distant mumbo jumbo. Yet, as Walter Kasper has argued, the 'grammar' of perfect love is summed up in the community of Father, Son and Spirit, and is *the* Christian answer to the God-question. When Joanne began to pray with a sense of Trinity, she was arriving at what is specifically Christian. In my experience this appreciation is not beyond our grasp, nor for theologians only. It is something quite simple. The gospels more than once tell us of Jesus being led by the Spirit and of his praying to the Father on the mountain. As Joanne discovered for herself, when we pray, we enter into and echo that encounter: we are invited to turn *towards* the Father, *with* Jesus, and so to pray *in* the Spirit. We have then a rich and threefold answer to our question, Where is your God? God is *beyond* us; God is *beside* us; God is *within* us. Or to come back again to our Magi metaphors, God is in the silent adoration, and in the giving, and in the dream.

Choosing to Give

The moment of the Magi story most frequently shown in art is the presentation of gifts; it is usually depicted as an exotic scene in keeping with the rich gifts listed by Matthew.

Once again we can approach the episode as capturing an essential strand in Christian living: we are here to give of what we have been given.

Where do we learn generosity of heart? What forms does it take in different circumstances? Perhaps the transparent generosity of the saints has always helped to make sense of faith. Even our confused culture is moved when it glimpses God through the extraordinary goodness of ordinary people.

PEDRO PABLO

Many of the stories told about people in these pages use changed names, and some disguise the identities still further in order to avoid embarrassing the real people in question. On this occasion, however, I will use no such disguise or change of name. It is most unlikely that the young boy concerned will ever see these pages. He is living in a poor *barrio* in Venezuela, but if by chance this book were to be translated into Spanish, I would be delighted for him to read about himself. He might even have forgotten the incident. I will never forget it. It was something that summed up – in

one eloquent but simple act – the spirit of giving which is
found in the gospels.

It happened like this. In 1987 I was spending some time
in San Felix, a city in the east of Venezuela. I was staying
with a Jesuit community living in the middle of a large *barrio*
with some 40,000 people in this one parish. Conditions were
pretty basic. Some were living in huts and others had
developed their huts over the years into what in Ireland
might be called brick cottages. At the time of my visit, there
was a shortage of tap water – in spite of the fact that we
were beside the huge Orinoco river. The contrast of two
worlds never hit me more than one morning when I wanted
to wash. The only tap water was an inch or so scooped from
our communal barrel, and this had a few dead flies in it. As
it happened my bit of soap had 'Japan Air Lines' on it. The
comedy of it seemed to point to the tragedy of our divided
planet. I could remember sipping sake in that luxurious
plane, and here I was washing in an inch of dirty water.

Across from our community lived a very poor family with
many children. There were two mothers and about twelve
children under the one roof. I never saw the fathers – they
were away looking for work in another part of the country.
One of the children, a boy of about eleven called Pedro
Pablo, used to come across to our place fairly often, sometimes to see if any spare mangos had fallen from our tree
during the night. (They used to thud on the tin roof and
wake me up!) He became friendly with me. For him I was
something of a novelty – so white and unable to speak
Spanish properly. We arranged to exchange lessons because
he was beginning to learn English at school. This particular
day the children were all sent home from school after an
hour or two, because without water they had no toilet facili-
ties. So Pedro Pablo came over to me as my teacher and
pupil. We were swopping simple words like 'hand' and 'tree'
when I noticed that he was continually rubbing his stomach

under his shirt. I asked him 'Tienes hambre?', 'Are you
hungry?' He nodded a bit shyly. When had he last eaten?
Yesterday morning. Was there nothing in his house?
Nobody had anything to eat except a few mangos. I asked
him if he would like a big sandwich. Again he nodded, a bit
embarrassed. Although we had not much in our kitchen, we
had the makings of a sandwich. But when I made it and
gave it to him, he didn't eat it. 'Aren't you going to eat it?'
I can still remember his reply in Spanish and I think the
words will stay with me for a long time. 'Voy a llevarlo a
mi mamá que está embarazada.' 'I'll bring it to my mother
who is pregnant.' And off he went, leaving me stunned. I
sat there for a long time in silence.

Comment seems superfluous. Perhaps for the reader it
cannot have the same importance it had for me. I sensed
that I had glimpsed Christ's spirit alive in a poor child. It
was one of those profoundly moving moments when one
feels in touch with the heart of life, with the reason for being
here at all. It is good to add that the story did not end there.
Pedro Pablo's generosity was contagious, and I found myself
able to arrange that, at least for those days, there would be
no more hunger in that household. That may have been a
happy ending in the small scale of one family and in the
short term of a few weeks. But what of the larger cry of the
majority of this hungry world? That needs a more imaginative giving, and a more uphill effort of change. And that too
is the call of the Kingdom now.

In this respect I think of that final and most radical of the
Kingdom parables of Jesus, the picture of the last judgement. It makes no mention of God, but only of loving
deeds or their absence, and it ends with a revolutionary
identification of Jesus with all the wounded of history: 'In
so far as you did this to one of the least of mine, you did it
to me' (Matthew 25:40). I recall seeing a cartoon of this
once, which in its own way captured a key aspect of the

parable for our time. There was a large court-house with 'Last Judgement' on the dome, and with many doors marked for various categories of sinners: robbers, adulterers, and so on. Over one door was written 'unbelievers' and out of this door a stream of people came jumping with delight. The caption read, 'Faith isn't on the exam paper'!

Ours is an unbelieving age. For all sorts of cultural reasons there is a crisis in the language of faith, more than in faith as such. Many people find themselves victims of uncertainty over many things, faith included. This would apply to most of the students I have known in recent years; even when they held on to some of their inherited religion, they often remained unsure in matters of faith. Yet again and again I found them wanting to give of themselves in some way. It is as if faith is a chord with several notes, and the note that rings strongest within today's culture is the note of offering one's gifts. That moment in the Magi story sparks off a secret generosity within many a young person, even when s/he cannot in all honesty make sense of other notes in faith. If these generous desires remain latent or even secret, it is often because they have not been recognized or called forth into action. In terms of the Magi imagery, it is as if nobody comes with the key to their coffers: 'opening their treasures, they offered him gifts'.

ANOTHER TEENAGER

Several years ago, when living in the United States, I became acquainted with a family of Irish origin. Among the children was one who was looked on as wild and troublesome – a sixteen-year-old boy. Let us call him Sean. A crisis arose while I was there; he was diagnosed as suffering from venereal disease. As an outsider and a priest – and as somebody whom he related to a little – I was asked to speak to him. Not the easiest prospect but to my surprise Sean took

the initiative, and asked me to come to his room. Once
there, our dialogue went in an unexpected direction. He
produced a poem that he wanted me to read, and which he
later gave me as a present. Part of it went as follows:

> They think I'm just a piece of dirt
> as my father said to me;
> it seems that I don't care a damn
> for anyone but me.
> But they don't know the hopes I have
> locked up inside of me,
> they never ask about the poem
> I'd like my life to be.
> If they saw this, they'd sneer and mock
> 'cos the me they choose to see
> is the cause of this whole family shame –
> true, but only part of me.
> But what I want, after all this mess,
> is that some day they will see
> that I do care and seek out my space
> to live and give and BE.
> I want a different sort of life
> not one of simply me,
> not grabbing but giving of myself
> Christ-like and tenderly.

It may be unsure as verse but it is real as a cry from the
heart. It expresses a longing for recognition of his generosity, something deeper than all the hurt and guilt. That secret
self can remain under lonely lock and key until somebody
offers a word of recognition – as I was able to do. Indeed
later that evening I managed to have Sean show some of his
poems to his father and mother. It was a healing moment
when he read one of them (not this one) aloud, and I could

see a strange pride in the eyes of his parents: their Sean was something other than a shame and a trouble-maker.

This may seem romantic and soft. Perhaps. I am simply witnessing to my constant experience that behind bad news good news often lurks. Behind the criminal, the rapist, the murderer, the addict – and I have met them all – a basic generosity waits in secret, and has never been quenched. One could put all this in more exalted language and speak of fundamental options that people live by. Is anyone wholly evil? I doubt it. Everyone falls into shames and guilts of various kinds. Some cause terrible pain to others. But the flow of each life is a tussle of options, between grabbing or giving, as Sean's poem put it. Or, as he also said, between not caring a damn, and struggling to live 'Christ-like and tenderly'. Perhaps this is *the* image of Christ that speaks to our present culture – the sense of someone completely for others, a life totally given. Many people, like Sean, may remain blocked or distant from the fullness of faith – from church, prayer, or any much understanding of the gospel. But they are seldom without this hunch of the heart that the greatest goodness shone in Christ, and that somehow they too want to live that way.

What happens to this desire in practice? There can be a painful gap between generosity hoped for and generosity lived. Pre-Christian philosophers, like Plato, recognized that nobody actually chooses evil, and that anybody can be deceived into choosing false good. This is where, in our story, Herod and his agents are at work, seeking to limit those hopes of Sean, or of anyone, to the level of mere desire. Fruitless wishes do no damage to Herod's system. Christians, however, are realists about the struggles entailed in living out the goodness in each person. That is where they see two crucial forces enter the human fray: the Church and the Spirit. We have already seen how isolation weakens resolve and how community is vital to stay on the wise way.

Christians also believe that the Spirit is at work in all hearts, like a slow sculptor shaping beauty from hard rock. This will be the focus of our next section, where we come to the Magi's 'dream'.

The Dream and the Spirit

There is no indication in the Magi story that they would not have returned to Herod with the news about Bethlehem, were it not for the dream. Humanly they had been deceived by him – so much so that it took a direct message from God to alert them to the falsity. About this we are told only that they were 'warned in a dream' not to return to the king. We do not know the precise content of the dream.

In the Bible dreams are frequently the way in which God speaks to people from within. The dream of the Magi was how they were guided by the Spirit and protected from dangers.

How can this happen today? Does revelation continue? Where do people find wisdom to see through the sham? How are we guided now in the key decisions on our journey?

THE LANGUAGE OF COMMITMENT

James Fowler in his book *Stages of Faith* makes a crucial distinction between the faith capacities of a teenager and those of a young adult. The teenager lives an adventure of relationships and in this way establishes his or her sense of identity. So the faith language characteristic of the late teens involves an interpersonal awareness of God. Even though it may remain shy and inarticulate, Christ is imaged as some kind of friend. But when one enters the twenties, another potential emerges: a faith based more on decision and lived out as a commitment, even against a tide of social pressures. Where the teenager will follow the crowd, or need to find support within a community of peers, the young adult is better able to stand on his or her own feet. Where previously the typical pattern was one of changing relationships, at this time the possibility of marriage becomes real. The young adult is also able for a faith rooted in choice rather than relying on the solidarity of some group. If Fowler's insights hold good, as I believe they do, it means that there is an invitation in our humanity to expand our language of faith as life progresses. In this way faith, though rooted in God, becomes a long adventure of human change.

I have noticed something of this transition from adolescence to adulthood many times during my years of university work. The personal issues raised by the younger students, especially those in their first year, were often connected with relationships or friendships. Typical concerns were with parents or loneliness or self-image or intimacy. But by the time students arrived at their third year, things had often changed. Their focus now became some variant on 'What am I going to do?' or 'How do you go about making a decision?' The shift of agenda may be due in part to the looming reality of life-beyond-study, but it is also connected with that transition in human development, which Fowler highlights, from a phase of relating and belonging to being able to decide and commit oneself in a new way. The theologian Bernard Lonergan stresses that this is a crisis point in a person's freedom, when she or he finds out that it is up to her- or himself to decide what to make of that self: 'Freedom decides what freedom is to be. The opposite is drifting.'

Since in today's culture there is so much less support for faith than a generation ago, this capacity for commitment has also become a vital area for religious formation. It is crucial to help people, first to awaken to the need for faith-as-decision and then to have the steadiness to carry that decision through into life. In terms of our Magi model, it is a matter not only of trusting the light and surviving the darkness but of seeing through Herod's pressures and resisting them. Then and only then could good decisions be made.

In their case this level of wisdom came through a dream, which can symbolize the deep self where God speaks to people from within. It is an image of how God 'even at night directs my heart' (Psalm 16:7). Just as the star offers a positive invitation to search, the dream serves a more negative role of discerning the deceptions. Even in everyday speech, we say about some problem that it is good to 'sleep on it', and often enough we wake up clearer on an issue than when we went to bed. It seems that the Magi visited their underworld in sleep and that in those strange depths the Spirit was able to show the 'world' of Herod to be wrong (John 16:8). But perhaps the dream level has further significance for faith. It is a zone of self-communication beyond the limitations of everyday consciousness. It is beyond language; instead, it exploits the richness of the imagination. It is beyond the practicality of the left-hand brain; instead, it liberates the right-hand logic of intuition. It is beyond the externality of the waking self; instead, its wisdom comes from another wavelength. And in this biblical example, it seems also to be beyond a merely human wisdom; instead, it is a space of revelation where they are guided to 'the complete truth' (John 16:13), or to adapt the words of St Paul, it is an instance of how 'the Spirit joins himself with our spirit' (Romans 8:13).

STRUGGLES OF CHOICE

How can we make decisions rooted in faith? How do we get in touch with the level symbolized by the dream? How in practice do we experience the guidance of the Spirit? I will take two contrasting examples to illustrate this process of decision-making in a horizon of faith. The story of Tony will flesh out the actual process of making a major choice, while that of Karen shows what may be needed before the time is ripe for any decision-making. Even from mid-teens Karen was a conscientious searcher for spiritual values to live by. Brought up in a fairly religious family, she conformed to her parents' expectations of church practice even through periods of unease and distaste. She always believed in God, but this God was a somewhat stern judge who induced guilt and remained distant from her confusions. Luckily she managed with the help of a good retreat experience to overcome some of these particular blockages and to ground her faith in a sense of Christ. This came about for Karen through learning to pray the gospels more personally; in this way she emerged from her childhood models and found a more nourishing basis for faith during her late teens. So far her story was a classic one of moving beyond a merely inherited belonging or conformity into an interpersonal language of faith. My contact with Karen came at a later stage – when at the age of twenty-one she was beginning to wonder about choices and even about the possibility of a special vocation. It seemed a genuine question, in tune with her prior experience, but whenever she tried to think it through, she kept coming back to me with litanies of self-complaint. She was getting nowhere. She didn't seem able to do anything steadily; she seldom prayed any more, and gradually dropped any regular church-going. Nevertheless there was a strong faith there, and a high idealism about serving Christ, especially awoken by the pain of others. Karen often spoke of being moved by people on the margins of society – dropouts, people with AIDS, addicts. But what she called her 'unsteadiness' continued and she felt blocked over any decision. She experienced no lasting peace – which I had suggested as a key signal of a good decision. For my part I did not know what might be troubling Karen or defeating her hopes. Then one day a simple light dawned for both of us. I was summarizing some of my impressions of her generosity, and at one point asked her how she felt about it. Karen's response was immediate, if a bit embarrassed: 'I don't think I was listening really. I can't take praise. I just turn off and go back to being preoccupied.'

It was a most revealing moment and indeed a turning point. From pausing on that honest answer, we discovered at least two enemies to the ripeness needed for a decision. The first was that she thought of herself as a fraud, never able to satisfy the perfection expected of her. Expected by whom? By parents and by a parental kind of God: this of course is a paraphrase of a longer conversation. And the second source of unreadiness came from the fact that she had hardly any close friendships and none at all with men. In short, Karen was handicapped through an excessive perfectionism and a lack of intimacy with peers. We had been barking up the wrong tree so to speak. Or we had been pushing the wrong door. Before she could come to the threshold of a good decision, and especially one that might involve a life choice, Karen needed to work on those two areas. Dismantling the oppressive and parental voices (internalized voices, not necessarily her real parents) was something that could be talked through with me or with anyone whom she found helpful. My own hunch was that once this liberation from self-negatives was underway, the second area would take care of itself in time and with a little courage to risk reaching out. And so it has been. Karen's journey towards new confidence has gone through a few years of slow and undramatic expansion. She has stopped being crippled by the judging ghosts, as she calls them, even though they can still haunt her in small ways. She is gradually finding herself able for deep friendship of various kinds. Her story remains incomplete as I write. It is a story of quiet struggle and honesty. It is a story of generosity that had to pause and grow before finding its true language. Recounted here as a summary of just one person's search, it highlights the uniqueness of each life as a mixture of fragility and strength. As with Karen, decisions are seldom made smoothly; they may require prior tackling of various unfreedoms within a person. But a good decision is surely worth whatever struggle is involved.

THE STAINED-GLASS EXERCISE

Tony's situation was different. It was a question of a marriage choice and more particularly of a certain confusion of feelings at the prospect of announcing an engagement to Helen. There was no doubt in Tony's mind that their relationship was the best he had ever known, that a marvellous companionship had grown up between them. But was this love? Did they really share the same values? Could they risk the big yes of marriage? These and many other questions began to plague him as the time of decision approached. It had already been agreed privately between them, but going public was a more fearful step, for Tony at least. Suddenly small things gave rise to conflict, such as how they would tell their parents, or whether or not to have an engagement party. Tony came to talk things over with me and after a while it seemed clear to both of us that although he was probably just suffering from nerves, it would be worthwhile to listen to the message of his feelings.

Since Tony was a firm believer (and in fact had spent some time in a seminary), my suggestion was that he approach his decision-making in a prayerful spirit, looking on the marriage choice as a vocation. I offered him my own brief definition of a vocation as a 'willingness that stays happy'. It may be short, but each word counts. A vocation needs the three ingredients: a willingness to give one's life in this way, a capacity to stand the test of time, and its genuineness will be shown in fruits of peace and joy. One might object that my definition makes no explicit mention of faith: I take that for granted and assume that it is through our humanity that the Spirit most often works and speaks.

More concretely I proposed a 'stained-glass window' exercise to Tony. He was to imagine himself in a room with two stained-glass windows. One of them depicts his own future as married to Helen. The other shows him married to another woman or living his future in some other way. First of all, he was to spend time praying for openness, realizing that God is active in his life, and asking to know and respond to whatever might be best. Next I asked him to give at least half an hour, separately, to entering into each alternative. Indeed, he was to take the two parts of this exercise on different days, thus letting the mind rest on the issues even outside the exercise proper.

So on the first day Tony was to enter into a fantasy of being married to Helen, and on the next day he was to envisage alternative futures as right for him. In each case he should give freedom to his imagination and pause wherever he found his feelings touched. He was to seek the positive reasons and emotions in each possibility. As each picture developed and filled itself in, he was also to pray for the light of God to shine through the glass, so to speak. Or, to change the metaphor, he was to hold the Geiger counter of himself and his responses over each alternative, allowing the implications of each choice to sink in. By being aware of his feelings as well as of the more objective pros and cons, he could watch the needle of that Geiger counter of the self. Then on the third day he was to come back to prayer and to weigh before God which of the two alternatives spoke more powerfully to him or left him with more lasting peace. Where was there a stronger sense of rightness? Described in this way, the whole thing may seem strange and elaborate. Its strength and wisdom is that it avoids the confusions of 'on the one hand', 'but on the other hand'. This constant to-and-fro reminds me of people following the ball at a tennis match, and in decision making it is counter-productive. But with the suggested method of discernment, there is time to listen with the heart, and in prayer, to both sides, before coming to weigh the two responses.

In Tony's case it turned out to be simple. Approaching the question in a prayerful spirit, he found that when he envisaged being married to someone other than Helen, it appealed only to his 'adolescent self', as he called it. When he tried to imagine other possibilities, such as a religious vocation, he again found that it was attractive but not for him. On reflection, he began to suspect that his unease over the marriage commitment might have been provoked by an unresolved guilt over leaving the seminary several years before. When he came to the 'window' of marriage with Helen, the sense of rightness was unmistakable, and further blessed with a deep gratitude before God. Clearly, in this case there was little need for the weighing of issues planned for the third day. But it was wiser to do it just the same, to protect the decision against later moments of insecurity.

As in other examples mentioned, Tony's discovery needed a deeper listening to his own experience than was possible under pressure. Like many a person faced with a major step in life, he was buffeted by a certain panic and by lingering self-doubts. His important insight was that within himself were two distinct levels of response, one mature and in tune, the other superficial and immature. It is the old contrast between the true and the false self in everyone, and what is called discernment simply means learning to read that contrast, to sift the levels, to recognize the roots in the light of the fruits.

THE SPIRIT AT WORK

When pondering the dangers of darkness in an earlier section, I mentioned the practical wisdom of Ignatius Loyola – about not changing direction in the dark. I want to draw on him again to cast light on this whole business of making decisions as a believer. In his *Spiritual Exercises* he assumes that the road to making a good decision will seldom be smooth and that it will require some preparing of the ground more often than not. If the heart is to be free, it will have to confront its unfreedoms. If I am to avoid the deceptions of the Herods inside and outside me, I will need some grace like the dream of the Magi. One of the simplest and most important assumptions of Ignatius is that God is at work within each person's experience, and that it requires only a careful listening and a certain liberation to become aware of the 'movements' of the 'good spirit'. For many people this is revolutionary. If they have grown up with a religion that keeps God distant or with a view of revelation as utterly over and done with, they will never think of God as acting *now* in their lives. If so, they will never trust their own deep experience as a place where the Spirit continues to speak and guide. 'Where is your God?' Yet another answer is possible: God is within you and can be recognized, where his Spirit and your spirit meet.

To say this is only to echo key moments in the New Testament. The night before he died, Jesus promised to his friends that he would be present to them in three new ways: in the bread and wine; in the love of one another; and in the coming of the Paraclete. This third gift is the one that Jesus spoke of most at the Supper, as if to stress that his absence would open the door to a new and deeper presence. Physically his friends will see him no longer. Spiritually this 'other Paraclete' will continue to be 'with' and 'within' them 'always' (John 14:16–17). Even the word *other* is revealing:

it implies that Jesus himself was the first Paraclete and that his work will continue in a new way. What then does this strange word Paraclete mean? In fact many things. Its root meaning is 'advocate', literally somebody called alongside to plead on one's behalf, like a defence lawyer in a trial. The whole setting in John's Gospel implies that the friends of Jesus are going on trial, that they will run into trouble in the 'world', but that they will have this attorney and witness to defend them and to guide them 'to all truth' (John 16:13). They will have a new consoler to encourage them and 'remind' them of Jesus (John 14:26).

Biblical experts have written volumes on these short passages but the core message is clear. It is that Jesus promises to continue to live within humanity in a new and real way – dwelling in each person through his Spirit. This is the basis of the confidence of Ignatius of Loyola that we can experience the movements of the Spirit, and that these will guide us towards good decisions. If the richness of this vision comes alive for a person, then religion changes its wavelength. It is no longer a matter of Church-belonging only or of duties to a distant God or of keeping commandments. All these have their place, but once the Spirit becomes real for a person, faith deepens into something at once personal and more than personal. In the depths of each self, to borrow an image from St Paul, we are being shaped into 'God's work of art', into the goodness that is meant to be 'our way of life' (Ephesians 2:10). The Spirit, as mentioned earlier, is that sculptor working away on the granite of our humanity, and it is possible to recognize the Spirit by its fruits: 'love, joy, peace, patience, kindness, goodness, trustfulness, gentleness and self-control' (Galatians 5:19–22).

This is what Ignatius called the experience of consolation as opposed to the experience of desolation, and although he expects people to run into conflicts where these two moods tussle together, he assumes that consolation will win and that it is the normal experience for a Christian. It is also the touchstone for any decision. If 'an inner joy calls and draws' one to goodness, and if it lasts, then, says Ignatius with disarming directness, we can trust that 'the good spirit guides us'. It is a startling claim for those who have never learned to trust their own experience as an answer to the question 'Where is your God?' But it is a liberating insight that translates the gospel promise of the Spirit into the individual experience of each person.

All this is simpler than the many words we use to explain it. I recall, with a certain comic embarrassment, an incident when I was studying theology. We had one professor, John Hyde, recognized by all as a man of both learning and sanctity and also as a man who hated eloquent frills of any kind. He taught a course on grace, and at the end of the year there was a fifteen-minute oral examination on the topic. I had put a lot of work into the course and thought I was well prepared. Hyde, as we always called him, quizzed me up and down and, seeing that I knew the areas reasonably well, threw in a deceptively simple question, 'What does grace do to a person?' I responded with the views of all sorts of authorities from Augustine to Rahner, from Aquinas to Schillebeeckx. To no avail. Hyde interrupted me on every route with 'But what does grace *do* to a person?' Eventually the clock ended my agony. 'Time up', he said with a certain satisfaction. 'Grace changes a person. Goodbye now.'

To return to the imagery of the Magi, the dream is what changes their plan; that is the moment of the Spirit's intervention to save them. Perhaps God intervenes only in ways like this – changing hearts through his Spirit, not working magic in an external way. For us too the dream protects us from Herod's lies and guides us towards to the love story that we are asked to live. We find, to our surprise, that the dream of God coincides with our own deepest desires. It is only to the false self – the self that Herod hypnotizes – that God seems an enemy. But when we reach the cave of our hearts, God's hopes and our hopes mingle and merge. 'Where is your God?' We can now answer in yet another way: where the two dreams meet, God's and ours.

Another Way: Justice

The last words of the Magi story – 'they went home by another way' – no doubt refer to their route back to the East and to the fact that they avoided returning to Herod. But in the poetry of the gospel 'way' seems to be a code word for the way of life that Christ called the Kingdom. It means a wholly different vision.

The Magi did not stay on in Bethlehem. They went back to their own country. The end of their story is not known, even though many legends have been woven around them. What can be gleaned is that they returned changed to their homes: they had experienced a journey of awakening. They now had a different sense of God, something to shape the rest of their lives. But we are left guessing as to how they continued to find God, or remain faithful to what they had discovered.

How can I live the vision of God that I glimpse in Jesus Christ? That is always a crucial question for faith but never more so than in our confused and crisis time. How can we find 'another way' for today?

MARTYRDOM

In November 1989 I received a letter from an old friend; it came like a gift out of the blue. Conor describes himself as an unbeliever. Yet he wrote to sympathize with me over the deaths of my fellow-Jesuits in El Salvador. 'Taking the side of the poor and powerless is obviously as dangerous as it ever was. I find it profoundly moving and humbling that men like these are prepared to die for their commitment.' Conor could have stopped there – with that generous tribute – but he did not. He went on to comment that 'it's terribly easy to criticize the diversity of opinion and stance which makes up "The Church" but there are still individuals within it who are genuinely Christ-like. They ask important questions of us all. I feel chastened and challenged.'

So do I, needless to say. In that spirit I want to respond here to Conor's letter, accepting of course his honest unsureness over faith. I'm not trying (and Conor knows this) to twist anyone's arm into faith, to argue them into some conversion to God. I'm simply talking out loud, so to speak – as if to myself in Conor's presence. Yes, I'd love him to discover the fragile but firm vision that is faith, but for the moment I'm simply taking his letter as a springboard for a final stage of wondering about the whereabouts of God.

Let me begin with what I call my '*entonces*' insight. That word is one of the most ordinary of terms in Spanish, and means 'then' or 'and so', with some sense of cause. But this little word was at the centre of an important insight that came to me on Friday the sixth of March, 1987. I was in Maracaibo in Venezuela, without doubt the hottest place I've ever been in my life. It was the first week of Lent (and my penance was the climate!). The Scripture reading for Mass that day (as every year) came from the prophet Isaiah, from chapter 58. It is one of those ironic passages where God, in the mouth of the prophet, is being sarcastic about how people get the wrong end of the stick about religion. 'They seek me day after day', as if they wanted to know my hopes, as if they were living as I ask them to. Yet they complain that they receive no reward, that they have no sense of my being with them. What is the point of penance or fasting, if I seem to stay so distant? But take a hard look at this so-called fasting. It's an external exercise, a pretence of penance – hanging the head and looking sad. But all the while workers are being oppressed, violence holds sway, and the poor are beaten up. (This is not an extract from some Amnesty International report but a close paraphrase of Isaiah.) The prophet goes on, speaking solemnly in the name of God: the real penance, and the one that I want from my people, is quite different. It would consist in liberating the oppressed, breaking the structures of injustice, lifting the burdens from the poor, sharing bread with the hungry, sheltering the homeless, clothing the naked, and not turning your back against your own people.

LIVE IT FIRST AND THEN . . .

What an extraordinary passage! But I have yet to come to my point. On that Friday in sweltering Maracaibo I heard that call to genuine 'fasting', as I had heard it many times before. Perhaps it had more drama for me because of being in Latin America. But I was not prepared for the impact of the next little word – *entonces* – and for what it led to. In Spanish the passage of Isaiah continues: 'entonces brillará tu luz como el amanecer . . . entonces, si me llamas, yo te responderé "aquí estoy".' '*Then* your light will shine like the dawn . . . *then*, if you call me, I will answer, here I am.' And the rest of the chapter develops that powerful promise. It is full of the word 'if'. *If* you struggle against oppression, *then* you will find God. *If* you create a world of caring, *then* all the old gloom and darkness will lift, and you will experience the closeness of God.

What came home to me was a surprisingly different angle on the quest for faith. Something utterly obvious seemed to fall into place as I listened to that familiar reading: not only is love more important than faith, but love is *the* gateway into faith. Confronted by Isaiah's words, I found that I was

putting the cart before the horse. I imagined faith to be
mainly a question of truth, a question for the mind. To think
things out may be vital, but it is not the key to faith. Isaiah
puts commitment to people first, and today that means
taking one's place in the struggle to heal our world. Previously I was inclined to interpret people's faith problems
as questions seeking answers, and to suppose that *after* a
person found faith *then* s/he could begin to live it. But that
'then' of mine is not the 'then' of Isaiah. For him faith is
more a form of love-truth than of reason-truth. The summary of his message would be: live it and you will know.
Live the option to serve the weak and the wounded, and
you will have fewer problems finding God. As Newman was
to put it centuries later, 'We believe because we love'.

In many ways my '*entonces*' insight is ridiculously simple
and far from new, but it had taken me half a lifetime to
grasp that the logic of faith is the reverse of what we are
used to: we normally know things by working them out and
verifying them. But faith is more an existential truth than
an objective one. It is verified in practice rather than in
theory. How I live in this world has a shaping influence on
how I see the meaning of everything. If I live uncaringly or
with self as an idol, then it is no surprise if God seems distant
or irrelevant. We meet God most, whether we recognize it
or not, through our lived options more than through the
gestures of our religiousness. The practices of religion, in
Isaiah's view, are authentic only when backed up with the
hard currency of action. It was such a stance and its cost in
El Salvador that moved Conor and gave him a sense of what
was 'Christ-like'.

THE PROPHETIC NOTE

The aim of many Old Testament prophets was to disturb
the status quo of the kings and priests, who settled too easily

for a religion of external observance. The prophets' goal was to rescue religion from its rigidities and to fire again the imagination of believers. Typically they would awaken people to God's hopes by reminding them of the sufferings of the poor. Perhaps I heard this emphasis in my youth, and certainly I must have read these biblical passages. But it has only been in recent years, and through the stimulus of being in Latin America, that these challenges have caught fire for me. As Marx liked to say, context conditions consciousness. My context of the individualistic West tended to keep faith within a largely private sphere. Until I saw the world of the poor with my own eyes – as opposed to the frequent images of Third World pain on television – I was able to avoid the vehemence of that prophetic note.

But once discovered this note sounded everywhere through the scriptures. To take just one example from the New Testament: I had read the letter of James many times but it was not until I read it prayerfully in San Felix – living opposite Pedro Pablo's family – that James's bluntness struck me with new force. Take the irony of his remark that even the demons believe in God (James 2:19). By comparing them to devils, James is satirizing believers who think that faith is an abstract truth, unconnected with how they live. On the contrary, he argues, without compassion it is a dead thing. His whole second chapter is a disturbing text for the complacent believer – which means most of us. Beware of treating people differently because of their social status. The poor have been chosen by God and are rich in faith. What use are kindly words towards those who are victimized? Unless you try to change their situation, your so-called faith is a hollow pretence. Don't just believe! Do something! Action is the only litmus paper for faith that James trusts, and the Conors of today seem to apply exactly the same test. They may remain shy of Church and suspicious of mere words, but they glimpse the truth of faith when it is lived in options of solidarity.

BY WAY OF SUMMARY

If the core of being a Christian means an alternative way of life, it also means a long battle with Herod – the Herod of ego within and of systems all around. Sometimes this option to live according to Kingdom values costs people their lives. Then, as Conor said, it becomes the strongest argument for faith. There is a relevant saying in John's Gospel that 'whoever does the truth comes out into the light' (John 3:21). We might adapt it for our contemporary situation of faith and doubt: what will most help those unsure, like Conor, to glimpse the light is the witness of believers who do the truth. For faith is less a theory than a commitment to share in the project which Jesus called the Kingdom – and that means a long transformation of hearts and of history.

Much energy and ink have been expended in defending God against atheism, and doing so on the level of theory. It is undoubtedly a useful debate, but sometimes little more than a debate. The more central question, in my experience, is not about the existence of God but about how faith can be lived in today's world. Credibility comes when livability is found, not the other way round. This book has been about people at various stages of that search for ways to live and about how God is encountered in their struggles and experiences.

So, finally, where is our God? What answers have we found? Several different and yet converging ones, all of them linked to moments in the Magi journey.

God is found through following the *light* that leads us into mystery. To find courage for that journey we often need some liberating awakening first – to the wonder of existence and of our own selves.

God is found even through the *darkness* that is unavoidable along the way. This need not damage us, if we trust that darkness is never the whole story and that we are never abandoned or alone in those shadows.

God is found by *questioning*, by honestly seeking to make sense of our experience. Some people get stuck with inadequate levels of questions and of answers. Yet, approached with reverence, there are avenues of inquiry worthy both of us and of God.

God is found while *walking side by side* along the road. We are not meant to travel alone. Faith blossoms through many kinds of community, and these are excitingly visible all around us today.

God is found in spite of *deceptions*, evils and dangers in our path. Although Herod's twisted system rules the world, to recognize his trickery is half the battle. Then we become free for another kingship.

God is found in the *house* that is the Church. For all its faults and failings, it offers a spiritual home, long tested by history. It is the place where the Spirit continues to guide the friends of Jesus, and where vast numbers of people find food for their journey.

God is found through *adoration* or prayer. We need simply to risk the strangeness of God's silence, where levels of deeper listening await us, and where the heart can learn a new logic of love.

God is found through *giving*. We are here for others, especially for the many wounded of our world. Anyone who tries to care in any way is not far from the Kingdom, and in the evening of life, says John of the Cross, we will be judged by love.

God is found through *dreaming*, whenever revelation touches the depths of a person. This conversion of vision can happen in many ways – through Scripture, through sacraments, or through the slow artistry of the Spirit, shaping hearts and changing lives.

God is found by choosing *another way* of living in this world. It means embracing reality and entering into the struggles of history, great and small. For the Kingdom is here as well as hereafter, and a Christian is someone who dances to that different tune, first powerfully heard in the heart of Christ and now echoed unsteadily in each life and in the larger drama of healing this world.

Where is your God? There is an Eastern parable which portrays God as playing hide and seek with humanity. According to one version, God asks the angels for advice about the best place to hide. Go to the farthest star. Try the depths of the sea. What about some inaccessible cave or desert? One angel more subtly suggests that God might find the best disguise among the poor. But eventually one wise old angel (or are angels ageless?) comes up with another idea. 'Hide at the centre of human experience, where the heart meets reality. Hide yourself at the cutting edge where people shape their lives.' According to the parable, this is the solution chosen by God.

I hope this book has been in tune with that tale. It too has tried to glimpse God in those places where people change and grow, where they let themselves be reached by the cry of others, where they listen and learn compassion, where they struggle and pay the price of love. Yes, God is there in the shaping moments of our human experience, at the turning points of our story, as the axis of our adventure in this world.

Epilogue

Several of the themes of this book are beautifully captured in a totally different medium, in Ermanno Olmi's *Cammina Cammina*. As I mentioned earlier, this is a unique presentation of the Magi story in a full-length feature film and one which brings a marvellous freshness to that familiar tale. Not only does it show the quest of the traditional three wise men; they are accompanied by their tribes on a chaotic pilgrimage that mingles reverence and irreverence. The heart of the film is both deeply spiritual (like Olmi's masterpiece *The Tree of the Wooden Clogs*) and gently satiric about what formal religion does to revelation. At the outset the young son of Mel, the Rabbi-astronomer, protests loudly against sacrificing a lamb as an offering to God, and throughout the film there are recurring moments of debate as to what kind of God they are searching for. At one point a strange, prophetic figure in the mountains mocks the pilgrims for seeking a god who would be their slave, whereas he is 'waiting for a God of joy, a friend'. The moment of finding Jesus with Mary and Joseph is handled with great tenderness; but immediately after Mel comments that people will wonder why God comes 'in such poverty', he holds a service of thanksgiving during which a collection is taken up among the crowd!

A little later, and with one of the shifts of mood typical of Olmi, one of the most significant conversations of the entire piece takes place between the interpreter (for the

Magi speak different languages) and Mel. 'Do you believe in God?', asks the linguist, adding that 'most people who believe in God have their eyes turned to the sky, but you're always looking at the earth'. Mel quotes a saying in response, 'Lift a stone and thou shalt find me. Chop wood and I will be there.' It is reminiscent of that comic moment at the opening of the Acts of the Apostles when the disciples after the Ascension are portrayed 'staring into the sky' and are rebuked by two divine messengers (Acts 1:10). The implication is that God will be found in reality, not in some purely spiritual realm.

But in what reality will God be found? That is the final source of conflict in *Cammina Cammina*. The three Magi have the same disturbing dream, and realize that 'the mighty in this world' will go to any lengths 'to stop people finding their King'. So they decide to leave for home, even if it means travelling through the night. But the interpreter bursts into angry protest against their self-concern, and offers another version of the significance of their dream. 'It's now that God is asking us for help.' In his view, they should go back to defend the child even at the risk of their own lives. 'God has no need of our help', says Mel in shocked response; his great plan is to build a temple to commemorate their discovery of the infant King. This scene enacts a perennial clash between two spiritualities, one of unworldly transcendence, the other of involvement in the struggles of history. The interpreter continues to insist that we serve God with more than 'words and signs'; so he rides back alone to try to save the child. He travels through scenes of carnage, with dead mothers and children strewn everywhere, until finally he comes to the stable where they had all seen Jesus with Mary and Joseph. Now there is nobody there, only a lamb bleating; but unlike the surrounding area, there are no signs of blood in the stable. The camera then switches to the Magi arriving home in triumph, and thus the films ends with ambiguity.

Is it enough to recognize God in Jesus, and then to celebrate that reality? Or are we to risk the danger zone in order to protect the child from Herod? Where is our God? Yet another variation suggests itself: where the visions of the heart and the struggles of reality meet and where that meeting gives life and bears fruit.